INTEGRATION AND DISINTEGRATION IN EAST AFRICA

Edited by
Christian P. Potholm
and
Richard A. Fredland

University Press
of America™

Library of Congress Catalog Card Number: 80-5914

To the Wananchi--

all of them.

iv

TABLE OF CONTENTS

PREFACE

The editors would like to thank the many Africans, Europeans and Americans who added to the findings and flavor of this work. Both were fortunate enough to have been able to do extensive field work in East Africa during and after the final months of the East African Community's existence. In this regard, Professor Potholm is most grateful to Dean Alfred H. Fuchs and the Bowdoin Mellon Fellowships Committee for their support and for a Fulbright-Hays Grant which enabled him to do field work in the area during 1977 and 1978. He would also like to express his thanks for the assistance rendered by Suzanne Theberge, Gladys Peterson and Linda Petrucci, as well as that of Liz Keohan and Jill Pingree, and Nizar Motani, currently executive assistant to the Aga Kahn.

Professor Fredland was the beneficiary of a sabbatical leave in 1977 which enabled him to conduct field research and to make use of the resources of the University of Nairobi. He is particularly appreciative of the assistance of Professors Vincent Khapoya and Domenico Mazzeo of the University.

Both editors would also like to thank the contributors to this volume who made just heroic efforts to meet both deadlines and shifts in emphasis. Scholarship truly is a collegial exercise.

Christian P. Potholm
Brunswick, Maine
1980

EAST AFRICAN COMMUNITY SERVICES

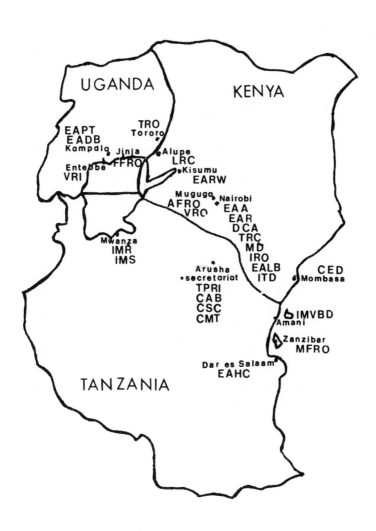

East African Community Services

		Location
AFRO	Agriculture and Forestry Research Organization	Muguga
CAB	Civil Aviation Board	Arusha
CED	Customs and Excise Department	Mombasa
CMT	Common Market Tribunal	Arusha
CSC	Community Service Commission	Arusha
DCA	Directorate of Civil Aviation	Nairobi
EAA	East African Airways	Nairobi
EADB	East African Development Bank	Kampala
EAHC	East African Harbours Corp.	Dar Es Salaam
EALB	East African Literature Bureau	Nairobi
EAPT	East African Posts & Telecommunications	Kampala
EAR	East African Railways	Nairobi
EARW	East African Railways Workshops	Kisumu
FFRO	Freshwater Fisheries Research Organization	Jinja
IMR	Institute for Medical Research	Mwanza
IMS	Inland Marine Services	Mwanza
IMVBD	Institute of Malaria & Vector-Borne Diseases	Amani
IRO	Industrial Research Organization	Nairobi
ITD	Income Tax Dept.	Nairobi
LRC	Leprosy Research Center	Alupe
MD	Meteorological Dept.	Nairobi
MFRO	Marine Fisheries Research Organization	Zanzibar
TPRI	Tropical Pesticides Research Institute	Arusha
TRC	Tuberculosis Research Center	Nairobi
TRO	Trypanosomiasis Research Organization	Tororo
VRI	Virus Research Institute	Entebbe
VRO	Veterinary Research Organization	Muguga

CHAPTER I

Introduction

Christian P. Potholm

With the overthrow of General Amin in 1979 by the combined efforts of the Tanzanian armed forces and Ugandan exiles, an era drew to a close in East Africa. During the previous decade, the once vibrant East African Community (EAC) disintegrated and Tanzania, Kenya and Uganda face the 1980's with feelings of concern and uneasiness. Assumptions about the nature and extent of regional unity were questioned, as were heretofore accepted norms of state behavior. Indeed, the whole question of the desirability of East African unity remains open as Kenya pursues an independent course of action in the face of growing Ugandan-Tanzanian reapproachment and what observers of the scene have termed "growing political alienation."(1)

Although the contributors to this work disagree on many facets of the past and the present, as well as the future, of the East African experience, all agree that it is essential to understand what led up to this period of instability, to ascertain what forces contributed to the decline of regional cooperation and to attempt to discover the extent of the "inevitability" of that decline. All insist that any predictions concerning the future of East Africa must be grounded in the knowledge of what preceeded the final breakup of the East African Community.

The initial impetus for this study arose out of a panel at the 20th annual convention of the International Studies Association, held in Toronto during March 21-24, 1979. Organized by Professor Fredland, "The East African Community: A Post-Mortem", brought together scholars from three continents who had either studied the Community in considerable depth or actually participated in its founding and its ongoing activities. Unlike many panelists, those participating in "The East African Community: A Post-Mortem," felt that there was a considerable enough degree of commonality in their findings to suggest that a number of important "truths" had been independently arrived at, and that the conclusions of the panelists should be made available to scholars elsewhere.

At the same time, all agreed that there were a number of additional dimensions which needed to be explored in order to put the East African Community's rise and fall in perspective and to insure that subsequent readers could be assured of a wider set of opinions as well as to be exposed to a number of political and economic findings which the original panelists had already digested in the process of doing their own research.

Integration and Disintegration in East Africa, therefore, incorporates the findings of seven different scholars whose views are often divergent but because each author read and made comments upon chapters of the other contributors, there emerged a considerable degree of commonality in terms of our findings, if only because the authors often agreed on what was not true, even if they could not always agree on what was true. In addition, although all contributors felt most comfortable focusing on the East African situation, an effort was also made to sift out the idiosyncratic elements so as to project the relevance of the East African experience for other regional groupings and the prospects for economic and political cooperation among states who share neither a common ideology nor a common level of development. In this regard, the editors hope that the entire work will be of interest even for those whose regional focus lies beyond Africa because the dynamics of bureaucratic politics, both within the individual states and within the Community as a whole suggests that these forces rather than the region in which they operated in many instances became the independent rather than the dependent variable.

In "Community Chronology," Allen Springer perceptively indicates the extent to which the Community actually represented over fifty years of regional cooperation and suggests the extent to which the colonial experience both knit the region together and also set in motion many of its most profound disequilibriums. For example, the presence of large numbers of white settlers in Kenya obviously had important impact on the political and economic history of that country, but it also influenced the timetable for independence and by stimulating certain kinds of development, tied Kenya into the international capitalist system to a far greater extent than either Uganda or Tanzania.

Moreover, Springer's analysis suggests that structural changes within the Community itself - such as giving the self-supporting services "corporate" status - impinged very directly on the ultimate outcome by increasing the momentum of bureaucratic activity quite apart from the wider diver-

3

gences caused by the differing political views held by the three governments. The dynamics of the Community's operations then, may well have exacerbated the existing national differences and made the task of regional conflict resolution far more difficult.

John Ravenhill also makes a similar point in, "The Theory and Practice of Regional Integration in East Africa," concluding that unfavorable political and economic structural factors may well subvert the arrangements such as the East African Community but also others as well. More controversial perhaps is his assessment that only more developed countries in regional settings can make the required sacrifices to make what he calls the "necessary side-payments" to the weaker partners in order to keep their interests high.

In addition, he points up the degree of the disintegration by indicating the extent to which the regional partnership in East Africa was more extensive than other such arrangements and that the set of institutional bulwarks might well have been expected to overcome many of the problems which subsequently sapped the strength of the EAC. Ravenhill is also interested in the apparent a priori necessity for regional groupings of this kind to make continual progress toward higher levels of integration in order to maintain momentum.(2)

For his part, Richard Fredland is concerned in his chapter with answering the question, "Who Killed the East African Community?" In examining a number of reasons given for the demise of the Community, he focuses on the unequal levels of development among the three member states, the divergent political and economic views of the ruling groups in Kenya, Tanzania and Uganda, the importance (or unimportance) of exogenous forces and the legacy of both the colonial period and "the first flush of independence" which undercut some of the more desirable aspects of integration by emphasizing the importance of political sovereignty. For Fredland, the most pre-eminent of these are the dominance of the Kenyan economy and the internal considerations which forced (or allowed them to be forced) the ruling elites in all three countries to place their national priorities and demands ahead of those of the total community.

4

Fredland is also interested in the possibilities that present themselves now that the Community has expired. Will other regional groupings take its place? Will the recent OAU accent on the broader context of east and central Africa lead to a wider arrangement? And he remains convinced of the difficulty in trying to ascertain which is the more important prerequisite for integration, economic cooperation or a favorable political climate. He concludes that whatever else the East African Community may teach us, it does not conclusively answer the integration prerequisite question.

"Problems of Regional Cooperation in East Africa" by Domenico Mazzeo goes at the problem from a somewhat different perspective. While concerned with the causes for the decline of the EAC, Mazzeo endeavors to put the process of regional integration and cooperation in the context of wider development strategies such as intercontinental cooperation and agreements between countries in the industrialized North and the often unindustrialized South.

He also branches out to discuss the consequences of the collapse of the East African Community to each of the participants, concluding that in the short run at least, the loss of the common market opportunities hurt Kenya the most while Tanzania and Uganda seem to have lost more from the termination of the financial and technical institutions. For Mazzeo, the new realities which follow both the decline of the EAC and the forced retirement of General Amin make it likely that Tanzania and Uganda may work to develop alternative infrastructural ties and thus ultimately reduce their dependence on Kenyan transportation facilities. He sees the most dangerous consequence of these events in the possibility of a regional arms race with Kenya feeling surrounded by ideologically imcomparable regimes and at the same time forced to cooperate with Ethiopia in the face of possible Somali irredentism and the flexing of Tanzanian military might in the aftermath of their successful war against Uganda.

Arthur Hazlewood brings to his chapter, on the "Economic Instrumentalities of Statecraft and the End of the EAC," broad experience in the region, both in the crafting of the Community treaty itself and as an observer/participant during much of its life. In his chapter, he asserts that it was the failure of the policy instruments which were introduced to satisfy the member states which was the fundamental reason for the disintegration of the East African Community. At the same time, Hazlewood takes exception to the notion that any treaty instruments could have in and of themselves solved the various problems which developed as the Community matured.

In his words, "the heart of the matter" is that when the member states put together the Community, it was their perception that the outcomes would be positive for all but that as time went on, the members began to see the likely outcomes as zero-sum games or even negative-sum ones. For Hazlewood, the Community was not killed, it faded and died from a lack of interest in keeping it alive. And it was the perceptions about the nature of the Community, as much as the realities themselves that caused the member states to take such a stance.

The nature of perceptions is very much central to my chapter, "Who Killed Cock Robin? An Analysis of Perceptions Concerning the Breakup of the East African Community." In it, the central focus is on the national actors and the views they held concerning the reasons for the breakup. Ideological differences, the failure of political leadership, economic realities, foreign intervention, changing times and bureaucratic rivalries have all been widely advanced as reasons why the Community collapsed.

I was primarily interested in the groups which held one or another reason as being critical in the Community's decline and in the chapter I suggest some of the reasons why one group held one view and another some other. In addition, it is my view that the failure of political leadership is more central to the collapse of the Community than many of the participants or observers indicated.

The question of perceptions would also seem to be of considerable importance in determining the future of regional relations. While many in the Organization of African Unity may feel that there is an opportunity in the collapse of the EAC to put together a bigger and better regional organization, perceptions about what went wrong and what would have to be done to get the three countries to even consider going down the integration path clearly differ.

Hrach Gregorian examines the period following the break-up of the community and the war between Tanzania and the Uganda of General Amin. "Plowshares into Swords: The Former Member States and the 1978-1979 War" analyzes the forces which led to the war and seeks to explain why the war had an outcome so few observers would have predicted. In addition, he examines the strains and tensions within the great African community as one Africa country invaded another for the expressed purpose of overthrowing its government.

Given the history of assassination attempts and the intrusion of exogenous elements through military coups, such an invasion may only differ in terms of the degree of involvement of the initiating country, but from a perceptional perspective, most member states deplored the precedent set by Tanzania, even though many were privately pleased with the outcome of the Tanzanian effort.

Nevertheless, in terms of East Africa per se, the continuing presence of 20,000 Tanzanian troops in Uganda and Tanzanian-Ugandan efforts to develop new infrastructural alternatives to Uganda's previous dependence on Kenya may well mean that any possible attempts at reintegration in the area will be years away.

In his conclusion, Richard Fredland wraps up this volume by indicating his observations on the preceeding chapters and summarizing both the elements of commonality and those of divergence before extrapolating current trends in the region in order to give a sense of where the region may be heading. He also suggests some of the relevance of the East African Community's rise and fall for regional groupings elsewhere. A select bibliography and background information on the contributors to this work follow his final chapter.

Chapter I

Footnotes

1. Anthony J. Hugues, "Disunity in East Africa," _Africa Report_ (November-December, 1979), pp. 4-10.

2. While not precisely addressing his issue, D. S. MacRae indicates the extent to which economic forces as well as the demands of the Kenyan economy set in motion forces which now seem to have worked rather continuously to increase the Kenyan productive sector. See D. S. MacRae, "The Import-Licensing System in Kenya", _The Journal of Modern African Studies_, Vol. XVII, no. 1 (March, 1979), pp. 15-28.

CHAPTER II

Community Chronology

Allen L. Springer

INTRODUCTION

The East African Community (EAC) was certainly not the product of a sudden burst of political inspiration in 1967. In many ways, it reflected the experience of over fifty years of regional cooperation first promoted by the British Colonial Office and later viewed by African leaders during the transition to independence as the basis for East African federation. Both the substantive obligations accepted by the parties to the Treaty for East African Cooperation and the institutions established to run the Community were a direct outgrowth of this experience.

This chapter attempts to place the EAC in a historical perspective. It examines the evolution of East African cooperation from the informal mechanisms created by colonial officials through the formation of the East African High Commission and the unsuccessful attempts of the early 1960's to unify the region under a central government. After focusing briefly on the treaty itself, our attention is then directed to major developments in the life of the Community and the divisive issues whose cumulative impact led to the final collapse of the EAC in the summer of 1977. The approach taken here is narrative and descriptive as other chapters examine more closely the operations of the Community and the causes of its disintegration.

THE EVOLUTION OF EAST AFRICAN COPERATION

The Colonial Experience

British colonial rule was, as Thomas Frank asserts, "the most profound of the unifying factors in the East African region."(1) Ties forged with the Sultan of Zanzibar in the 1820's to enhance British influence in the Indian Ocean were expanded to serve a wide range of colonial objectives in the 1880's and 1890's in response to growing German interest in East Africa. By agreements signed in 1886 and 1890, Great Britain recognized Germany's control over Tanganyika in exchange for German acceptance of Britain's right to establish a protectorate over the Sultan's former possessions of Zanzibar and the mainland areas of what became Uganda and Kenya. Zanzibar was made a British protectorate in 1890; Uganda followed in 1894 and in 1895 much of Kenya was incorporated into the East Africa Protectorate to guarantee transportation routes to Uganda. Tanganyika came under British administration following the First World War when a defeated Germany surrendered her colonies to the League of Nations mandate system.(2)

Measures were taken to promote more unified administrative control over East Africa well before Britain acquired its Tanganyikan mandate. The Court of Appeal for East Africa was established in 1902, followed by a postal union between Kenya and Uganda in 1911. In 1917 a customs union was created. Three years later the East African Currency Board began issuing a single regional currency. This gradually became the standard for Tanganyika after its formal transfer to Britain and by 1927 the customs union had been widened to include the former German colony.

To help coordinate these cooperative efforts and to promote the economic development of East Africa, Britain relied until 1948 on an informal consultative system, the Governors' Conferences, of which the first was held in Nairobi in 1926. Some colonial administrators had advocated a far more centralized regional authority. Sir Robert Coryndon, Governor of Kenya from 1922 to 1925, envisioned a gradual transition to political federation through the creation of functional ties in key sectors of the East African economy, such as

11

transportation and communication. Coryndon's successor, Sir Edward Grigg, suggested a more direct approach. In a 1927 report to the Colonial Office, Grigg called for the "establishment of a central East African authority to control main transport services, the customs tariff, inter-territorial communication by land and air including posts and telegraphs, defence and fundamental research."(3) Further support for federation came from the Hilton Young Commission in 1929. Yet strong opposition from both white settlers and African residents of the territories, as well as concern expressed by the League of Nations Mandate Commission about the possible violation of the Tanganyikan mandate agreement which political federation might entail, caused a new Labour government to advocate a more conservative approach. The Governors' Conference became the basic integrative mechanism of the 1930's with a permanent secretariat to assist in the coordination of regional colonial policy. Despite the failure to achieve the political union favored by Grigg and others, administrative control was improved during this period by the consolidation of East African services in such areas as air transport, meteorology, and income tax collection.(4)

Following World War II, the federation issue re-emerged as the British government was forced to respond to renewed colonial pressures for imperial reform. Proposals were again made to give East Africa a strong central authority but in the ensuing debate differences between white settlers, black Africans, and an increasingly significant and vocal Indian community became evident over the crucial issues of representation in the proposed Central Legislature and the powers of the High Commission, the key executive body of the new organization. Not surprisingly, the system which was finally agreed upon was weaker than that originally envisioned, designed to pacify groups whose only shared perception appeared to be a distrust of centralization.(5)

The East Africa High Commission was a direct, if strengthened descendant of the Governors' Conference. Made up of the three territorial Governors and based in Nairobi, it met several times a year to determine policy for East Africa and, most important, to supervise the operation of an expanded network of common services. What distinguished the High Commission from its predecessor was its greater sense of collective identity as a regional body.(6) Though still composed of individuals whose primary responsibility lay in governing their respective colonies, the High Commission was aided considerably in developing an East African perspective by the growing body of regional expertise found in the secretariat headed by an administrator whose position and influence became increasingly important through the 1950's.

The potential effectiveness of the Central Legislative Assembly was limited from the outset by the controversy which surrounded its internal composition and by restrictions placed upon its legislative role under the British Order-in-Council which established it. As a body designed to provide a greater voice for the East African people in the operations of regional institutions, the Assembly was viewed with suspicion by black Africans who had seen proposals for racial parity among those Assembly members elected by the territorial legislatures replaced by a system of voting which would seem to ensure disproportionate influence for the white settlers who dominated the legislatures.(7) The Assembly's power was circumscribed in two significant ways. First, many areas of possible cooperative activity were beyond its legislative competence. Fixing of tariff and customs rates, regional planning, and industrial licensing were among the subjects on which neither the Assembly nor the High Commission was empowered to act. Where legislation could be passed, the Assembly could be overruled by the High Commission and, in some instances, the Commission could legislate without Assembly approval.(8)

Despite these limitations, the new system provided a needed impetus for functional integration in the common services. Both the self-contained services,(9) capable of generating sufficient revenues themselves to maintain operations, and the non-self-contained services,(10) which required financial support from the High Commission, experienced rapid expansion in the late 1940's and early 1950's. Among the major advances were administrative measures to integrate the system of harbors and railways, the creation of an East African Navy (a step of particular symbolic importance to those who hoped for eventual East African federation, even though the fleet was composed of only two ships) and the expansion of Makerere College into the University College of East Africa. Income tax regulations were standardized in 1952 and the difficult problem of distributing

customs revenues among the territories was temporarily resolved by the Customs Management Act of 1954.(11)

By 1960, however, both Colonial Office authorities and
East African leaders recognized that the High Commission was
in need of reform. Sir Jeremy Raisman was chosen by the Secretary of State for the Colonies in July of that year to head
a commission responsible for analyzing the strengths and
weaknesses of the existing system and proposing appropriate
changes. Though many factors contributed to the decision to
appoint the Raisman Commission, three stand out as particularly significant.

First among them was the growing resentment in Uganda
and Tanganyika of what were perceived to be the disproportionate benefits accruing to Kenya under the existing system.
Statistics on GNP growth, foreign investment, and interterritorial trade indicated a widening development gap within the
region due, at least in part, to the effects of the common
market and the policies of the High Commission. High pro-
tective tariffs appeared to subsidize the growth of the Kenyan economy, with its larger manufacturing base, at the expense of higher prices in Uganda and Tanganyika and the loss
of revenue from import duties as increasing Kenyan industrial
efficiency shut out foreign competitors. Equitable distribution of those customs revenues that were collected was hampered by the free movement of goods within the region. A
complex transfer form process had been devised to determine
the ultimate destination of imported goods but enforcement
proved to be a difficult task. Since the Customs Management
Act had made the place of "retention" the key factor in al-
locating the shares of collected duties, Kenya's status as
the primary conduit for international trade seemed to guarantee that its proportion of the dispersed funds would be un-
fairly greater. Similar complaints were lodged against the
operation of the income tax system.(12) Kenya's East African
partners were also concerned that the location of the High
Commission secretariat and many of the common services in
Nairobi not only brought increased employment to Kenya but
also made the organization take greater interest in the well-
being of the Kenyan economy.(13)

A second problem with the High Commission was its reliance upon territorial contributions for much of the revenue

needed to sustain the non-self-contained services. In addition to inequities created by a funding system that resulted in approximately equal contributions by territories at different levels of development, long-term planning was difficult since it was impossible to be certain that the necessary money would be contributed should one of the territories become unhappy about the quality of assistance being provided.(14)

The final and most immediate reason for systemic reform was the impending independence of Tanganyika. Under pressure from the United Nations Trusteeship Council, which exercised some supervisory authority over the British administration of Tanganyika,(15) the British had decided to speed up the timetable for Tanganyikan self-government. A colonial organization was clearly incompatible with the new order evolving in East Africa. An opportunity was thus provided to address the problems revealed by twelve years of regional cooperation under the High Commission and, in the process, to establish a more promising framework for East African integration.

Yet the federalist goals of East African leaders, like Tanzania's Julius Nyerere, could not immediately be realized since Uganda and Kenya were judged by the British to be insufficiently prepared for independence by the December 9, 1961, date set for Tanganyika. Needed was a transitional structure capable of preserving the common services until agreement could be reached on a permanent federal arrangement.(16)

Independence and the Failure of Federation

The structure upon which the territories agreed in June 1961 was the East African Common Services Organization (EACSO) which came into existence with Tanganyikan independence. The EACSO formally severed the link between East African integration and British colonial rule; replacing the High Commission was the Common Services Authority composed of the three elected leaders of Tanganyika, Kenya and Uganda. Four ministerial committees were created to assist the Authority and the Central Legislative Assembly was revamped to improve its legislative competence and responsiveness to local concerns. According to Frank, "The age of government by civil servants and technicians had drawn to a close"(17) as politicians assumed increasingly prominent roles in the operation of regional institutions.

More significant perhaps than these institutional changes were measures based upon recommendations of the Raisman Report to divide more evenly the benefits of East African cooperation and to provide the Authority with greater financial independence. The Distributable Pool was the instrument chosen to achieve both ends. Actually established shortly before the EACSO came into being, the Pool was funded from a fixed percentage of the customs and excise duties and corporate income taxes collected by each of the countries. One-half of the Pool's revenue was retained by the Authority to support the operations of the common services and the rest distributed equally among the three members. While the new system provided the Authority with a more dependable source of funds, which would aid long-term planning, the Commission that proposed it and the territories that accepted it clearly saw the Pool as a means to address the major complaint of Uganda and Tanganyika concerning the inequitable effects of the common market. Kenya's dominance in both revenue-producing areas ensured that it would be contributing far more to the Pool than the others.(18) Partial accommodation had again been made on the benefit distribution issue, although the location of the EACSO and most of the common services in Nairobi alone provided a basis for future disagreement.

The transitional role of the EACSO made its limitations acceptable to Nyerere and others for whom federation was the political objective. In agreeing to join the EACSO and by maintaining its ties to the East African Currency Board, Tanganyika had accepted distinct limitations on its sovereign powers.(19) As its East African neighbors achieved independence,(20) this calculated policy of self-restraint provided a political and institutional environment conducive to the discussion of far more concrete integrative steps. On June 5, 1963, the leaders of Tanzania, Uganda, and Kenya announced in Nairobi their intention to establish the "political Federation of East Africa" by the end of the year. While recognizing the value of the economic ties created with the EACSO, they criticized the "lack of central political direction" and declared that "the time has now come to create such central political authority."(21)

The optimism of the Nairobi conference was short-lived, however, as differences soon emerged within the working party set up to prepare a draft framework for August's full constitutional conference. Perhaps the most contentious, and undoubtedly the most fundamental area of disagreement was the degree of centralization to be built into the new federation. Uganda's desire to preserve its fragile internal unity and the fear of Kenyan control over regional institutions led Uganda's representatives to support a far looser arrangement than that favored by Kenya and Tanzania. Opposition from Ghana's President Kwame Nkrumah, who claimed that a strong East African federation would serve to fragment the continent, did nothing to improve the negotiating atmosphere. Whatever the reasons for the inability of the working party to reach an acceptable compromise,(22) the failure was clear by the end of 1963. The last session of the group was held in May, 1964. Although the vision of a united East Africa would be resurrected by various national leaders throughout the 1960's and 1970's (often, ironically, at times of greatest disunity), the dissolution of the working party ended all reasonable hope for immediate East African federation.

The inability to achieve the goals of the Nairobi Declaration brought both frustration and a new sense of skepticism concerning the existing system of regional cooperation. The chief target of criticism was not the EACSO whose lack of centralization had supposedly been a key factor encouraging federation. It was in the field of monetary policy that the most dramatic signs of disintegration became apparent. The East African Currency Board, a vestige of British colonial rule, had remained intact since independence due largely to Tanzanian willingness to forego the benefits of control over a national currency until permanent regional institutions could be established. Through 1964 and the first half of 1965, Tanzania's intention to create its own national bank became increasingly evident and in June 1965, it was announced that the three countries would establish separate currencies and national banks.(23)

During the same period, the de facto and largely unregulated common market also came under attack. Again, the major cause of dissatisfaction was the perception that its operations unduly favored Kenya. Growing Kenyan surplusses in interterritorial trade seemed to support this view even

if, as Hazlewood points out, the Tanzanian and Ugandan economies were expanding at a faster rate than that of Kenya
during the 1961-1964 period.(24) The Distributable Pool was
seen as insufficient to correct trade imbalances and the
system of industrial licensing, which had been continued
through the transition period to independence, had failed to
satisfy Tanzania's desire for a conscious regional effort to
promote industrial growth in all three countries.

In the face of Tanzanian threats to withdraw from the
common market, East African leaders met in Kampala in April,
1964 and again in Mbale in January of the following year to
take corrective measures. The emphasis of the Kampala-Mbale
Agreements was on encouraging industrialization in Tanzania
and Uganda to redress unbalanced trade relationships. Provision was made for expanding the output of the Tanzanian and
Ugandan branches of industries that operated in at least two
of the countries to reduce reliance on Kenyan exports. Se-
lected industries, such as those producing tires, bicycle
parts and fertilizer, were to be sited in specific countries
and a program of incentives was envisioned which would promote more equitable regional development in the manufacturing
sector. Of greater restrictionist potential was the creation
of a quota program which permitted a deficit country, under
carefully defined circumstances, to apply to a regional Quota
Committee for fixed limits on the imports of certain products
from a country in surplus. Despite the obvious dangers of
introducing such an element into a system designed to maintain the free flow of goods across national boundaries, the
provision and, indeed, the entire agreement was a pragmatic
concession by Kenya to the desirability of continued East
African cooperation.(25)

Initially, shifts in production by interterritorial
firms did occur and several new industries moved into the
countries designated by the agreement for exclusive production rights. Tanzania and Uganda were permitted to institute
quotas on such products as beer and galvanized iron. Yet
Kenya, perhaps disappointed by the impending collapse of the
common currency arrangements, never ratified the Kampala-
Mbale Agreements and soon undermined the industrial allocation provisions by permitting the establishment in Kenya of a
tire factory which should have been located in Tanzania.(26)
Tanzania's President Nyerere held Kenya responsible for the

failure of the agreement and in August 1965, Nyerere imposed unilaterally a series of import restrictions, including quotas, on Kenyan products. These measures clearly violated the terms of the pact and enhanced the perception of gradual East African disintegration which had become increasingly widespread after the failure of the three nations to agree on a plan for federation. Earlier developments, such as the 1961 break-up of the East African Navy and Uganda's decision in 1963 to withdraw from the East African Tourist Travel Association, might now be seen not as minor setbacks but as significant stages in the decline of East African cooperation.(27)

THE TREATY FOR EAST AFRICAN COOPERATION(28)

It was thus at a time of deteriorating relations that the three nations began the long negotiating process that culminated in the Treaty for East African Cooperation. In June, 1965, Kenya called for a reassessment of the existing regional system. While such a review, once requested, was mandatory under the terms of the Common Services Agreement, there was general recognition that the continuation of both the common market and the common services was in the interest of all three and that significant changes were required to make them work more effectively. In September, the three heads of state decided to appoint a commission headed by Kjeld Philip, a United Nations economist and a former Danish minister of Trade and Finance, to undertake a comprehensive study of the problems faced and to make recommendations concerning the legal and institutional arrangements most suitable for the region. Consisting of three ministers from each of the countries, the Philip Commission was a "vehicle for negotiation" rather than a dispassionate expert body,(29) and played a key role in bringing the parties toward the compromise finally reached with the signing of the Treaty on June 6, 1967.

The Treaty's most obvious achievement was to place within one framework both the Common Services and the Common Market.(30) The latter, for the first time, acquired a solid legal foundation. Though hardly integrated in any operational sense, their inclusion in a single treaty reflected the experience of the 1960's that, in Ghai's prophetic words, "one could not survive without the other."(31) Further evidence of the political realism that had taken hold since the days of the Nairobi Declaration was provided by the direct manner in which the Treaty addressed the crucial question of benefit distribution. The principle aim of the Community was stated in Article 2 to be "to strengthen and regulate the... relations of the Partner States to the end that there shall be accelerated, harmonious, and <u>balanced</u> development and sustained expansion of economic activities <u>the benefits whereof shall be equitably shared</u>."(32)

To achieve this goal, the Treaty went well beyond the Distributable Pool relied upon by the EACSO. Within the Common Market itself, the primary mechanism was to be the transfer tax, essentially a special kind of interstate tariff.(33) Representing a concession by Kenya with its favorable trade balance, the transfer tax could only be imposed by a country "which is in deficit in its total trade in manufactured goods with the other two Partner States" and only upon manufactured products "of a value not exceeding the amount of the deficit in trade in manufactured goods between the State which is imposing the transfer tax and the State of origin of the goods."(34) Other provisions of Article 20 put limitations both on the items to which the tax could be applied, to ensure that it would be used to promote the growth of domestic industry, and on the level at which the tax could be fixed, an attempt to prevent the replacement of East African exports from those outside the Community. That the transfer tax was designed as a temporary measure was underscored by the fact that any tax would automatically expire eight years after its imposition and that all such taxes would be revoked after the Treaty had been in force for fifteen years.(35)

The Treaty's second major equalizing measure was the creation of East African Development Bank (EADB) whose general purpose was to promote industrial growth within the region by providing financial and technical assistance for specific projects. The Charter of the EADB emphasized its redistributive function by declaring a key objective to be "to give priority...to industrial development in the relatively less industrially developed Partner States."(36) While the three countries were to contribute equal shares of the initial capital of the Bank, precise lending targets were established which called for significantly greater investment in Tanzania and Uganda than Kenya.(37) The parties also elected to continue the East African Industrial Licensing Council through 1973 or until a new system could be established and agreed to develop "a common scheme of fiscal incentives towards industrial development" to prevent disruptive competition for new foreign investment.(38)

The basic Community institutions differed little from their predecessors in the EACSO, although several new bodies were established to help consolidate regional programs.(39) Firm executive control was retained by the individual heads of state who collectively constituted the East African Authority. All acts of the Assembly required unanimous acceptance by the Authority to become binding. To assist the Authority, a new position was created, the East African Minister, of which there were three in the new organization. Each country was permitted to nominate one individual who would, in effect, hold the Community's portfolio within his country's cabinet. Though the Minister could perhaps be expected to promote a "Community" viewpoint on the EAC's executive level, a role analogous to that played by members of the Commission of the European Communities, his position was far less secure as he could be removed from office simply at the request of the state which nominated him. Furthermore, the Minister's advisory function within the organization offered little chance for as direct an impact on Community policy. However, given his Cabinet rank, he gained more direct access to national policy-making circles than European Commission members enjoy.(40)

Five ministerial Councils were also set up to provide executive direction to certain Community activities and to advise the Authority on policy questions within their respective spheres. The two of greatest significance were the Common Market Council with overall responsibility for monitoring the Common Market and resolving disputes over its operation and the Communications Council which was to supervise the activities of the corporations. Also on the executive level was the Secretary-General in charge of a Community secretariat serving both the Common Market and the General Fund Services.

Within the Common Services, the most important change

21

was to give the self-supporting services "corporate" status, which previously had been the case only with East African Airways. All four were now to operate according to "commercial principles" under the immediate supervision of a board of directors. In a move designed to encourage a more even distribution of common service benefits, the East African Harbours Corporation was set up in Dar es Salaam as an entity separate from the Railways Corporation (they had been united under the EASCO) while the East African Posts and Telecommunications Corporation was transferred to Kampala. The Railways and Airways corporations were left in Nairobi but, when the EADB was sited in Kampala and the Community headquarters in Arusha, at least a geographical distribution of the major Community services had been achieved. The position of the non-self-contained services was altered little by the Treaty. All Community services which required financial support were to obtain it from the General Fund. The Fund's revenue was to come from the same tax sources that had maintained the Distributable Pool although the fixed percentage contributions which had led to surplusses under the EASCO were replaced by a formula designed to ensure that the money collected would approximate authorized Community expenditures.

For those who had hoped for an expanded role for the Legislative Assembly as an East African counterweight to the strong control exercised by the nation-oriented leaders of the Authority, the Assembly was a disappointment. Its limited constitutional powers under the EACSO were largely unchanged and the Assembly was given little voice in the operation of the Common Market. Moreover, selection of the membership of the reconstituted body was left up to national governments, replacing the previous system of direct election by state legislatures. Not only might this limit the responsiveness of the Assembly to public opinion within the region, but it was also feared that those appointed to the Assembly would be more "docile" than their predecessors and less likely to bring a critical perspective to bear on the activities of the Authority. To the degree that the backbench politics formerly evident within the EACSO's Central Assembly were stifled by the new system, the Assembly's potential as an embryonic federal legislature was undermined. Ghai saw these developments as a definite "backward step" in the process of regional integration.(41)

Three judicial institutions were placed with the Community system: the Common Market Tribunal, the Court of Appeal for East Africa, and the East African Industrial Court. The Tribunal was designed to play the most direct role in Community affairs, either by hearing cases brought by member states concerning alleged violations of Common Market provision of the Treaty or by giving advisory opinion requested by the Common Market Council. This important adjudicative function was never adequately fulfilled; the Tribunal failed to resolve a single case. The position of the other judicial organs was more narrowly defined. The jurisdictional competence of the Court of Appeals continued to be determined by the laws of each state and the Industrial Court could only rule on disputes of an industrial nature.(42)

THE DECLINE OF THE EAST AFRICAN COMMUNITY-1967-1977

The fate of the East African Community was linked inextricably to the volatile world of East African politics. Although many of the problems faced during its ten-year existence reflected significant differences over Community policies and their economic impact, from 1971 on the Community and its employees increasingly became convenient targets for national leaders in matters often quite unrelated to Community operations. In many ways, it is remarkable that so many of its institutions continued to function as long as they did in a political environment frequently characterized by open hostility between the member states.

The first three years of the Community were perhaps the most successful. Despite inevitable problems associated with the transition to new organizational structures, the Assembly began to enact Community legislation and the Common Market Council resolved a number of trade disputes. Progress was made in such areas as the harmonization of industrial and monetary policy. The real question seemed to be not would the Community survive but whether it might be expanded through association agreements with Zambia, Ethiopia, and other neighboring countries which had shown interest in such an arrangement.(43)

23

The Community suffered a serious setback when General Idi Amin overthrew Uganda's President 'Milton Obote on January 25, 1971. Obote fled to Tanzania where President Nyerere branded the new Ugandan leader a "treacherous Army Commander" and his government "an illegal regime, which had no excuse for staging a revolution."(44) The gulf between Nyerere and Amin widened amid reports in Uganda of an impending Tanzanian invasion. Its impact upon the Community was immediate when Nyerere blocked Amin's appointments to top EAC positions. Despite the Tanzanian leader's belief that the Community could continue to function without Tanzanian recognition of Amin, Kenyan mediation was required simply to secure Nyerere's approval of Amin's nominees. Far more serious was Nyerere's refusal to convene the East African Authority with Amin in power. Not only had the Authority provided needed direction for Community institutions, but without it such basic operations as approving the EAC budget became more difficult. New procedures were devised to circumvent many of these problems but serious damage had clearly been done to the cohesiveness of the organization.(45)

The situation deteriorated in the fall of 1972 when Obote's supporters launched an attack on Amin from Tanzanian territory. The dispute was temporarily resolved by October's Mogadishu Agreement, but no direct reference was made in the pact to Obote's future in Tanzania.(46) Nairobi's East African Standard correctly identified what was to become an ongoing source of Ugandan-Tanzanian friction. "If Dr. Nyerere...insists on providing a haven for Mr. Obote it is doubtful if he will receive much in the way of cooperation from Uganda."(47)

Tension continued into 1973 and again spilled over into EAC operations as Tanzania and Kenya became increasingly apprehensive about the safety of their nationals employed by Community corporations in Uganda. With news of the sudden disappearance of Kenyan employees of the East African Railways Corporation, the tone of the East African Standard changed. Declared the Standard, "the tide of resentment and anger is rising against Uganda."(48) Community unions began to press for repatriation of Kenyans working in Uganda and boycotts of Ugandan goods and services were threatened. Amin, however, was able to satisfy the Kenyan government that steps were being taken to protect its citizens and in May,

24

1973, a second agreement was signed between Uganda and Tanzania by which Amin agreed to pay compensation for the deaths of Tanzanian nationals in exchange for far more explicit guarantees from Nyerere that Tanzania would keep Obote's activities under control. In the improved political climate, Amin called for renewed discussion of plans for East African federation with either Nyerere or Kenyan President Kenyatta to serve as the leader of the new state.(49)

Conditions within the EAC offered little support for Amin's proposal. By the end of 1973, Kenya's dominance in regional trade had actually increased since the Treaty came into force. This was due in large measure to the collapse of the manufacturing sector of the Ugandan economy under Amin's unsuccessful policy of "Ugandanization." The Industrial Licensing Council had failed to promote the growth of efficient regional industries and was not renewed in 1973. In the monetary field, exchange controls first introduced by Uganda in 1970 and reciprocated by Tanzania and Kenya a year later had made monetary transactions more difficult. Although frequent consultation by the Governors of the three central banks helped to mitigate some of the negative effects of these restrictions, the new arrangements represented a significant departure from the degree of integration achieved earlier under the East African Currency Board.(50)

It was within the corporations, particularly the East African Railways Corporation, that some of the most immediate problems arose. Competition from increased road traffic in Kenya cut into the Railways' income during a period of high expenditure and, in late 1973, Tanzania began to hint that it might establish its own railway system. At the same time, Uganda and Tanzania began withholding funds which should have been transferred to the EARC headquarters. Shortages of foreign exchange following OPEC's quadrupling of the price of oil played a role in the funds transfer problem as did dissatisfaction with the policies of the Nairobi-based corporation. Under pressure from worker strikes in the summer of 1974 and rapidly rising fuel costs, negotiations began to decentralize EARC operations. East African Airways also came under close scrutiny by the Legislative Assembly in a 1973 report which criticized both its route selection and management policies.(51)

Transport issues resurfaced in a somewhat different context late in 1974. On December 2, Tanzania announced that its northern roads would be closed to heavy trucks, thus effectively curtailing Kenya's profitable overland trade with Zambia. Although Tanzania claimed that the measure was justified by the need for road repairs, Kenya issued a strong protest and retaliated by closing two border roads and interrupting steamer traffic on Lake Victoria. Pressures mounted in Kenya for the expulsion of Tanzanians working in Community corporations after reports indicated that as many as 1,000 Kenyans had already been deported from Tanzania. Meetings between Kenyan and Tanzanian leaders in December temporarily improved the situation and Kenya reopened the border on January 2. In a conciliatory speech to the East African Legislative Assembly, Nyerere insisted that Tanzania was committed to preserving the Community and warned against allowing short-term problems to undermine the vital role it could play in East Africa.(52)

The unwillingness of EAC members to transfer funds to corporate headquarters continued to plague the Community. In February 1975 all passenger rail services were stopped in Kenya and Uganda when the United Kingdom refused to supply any further spare parts until the EARC repaid its substantial debts. The fact that Tanzania was able to keep its own passenger trains running through the purchase of parts from Canada did little to enhance the prospects for resolving interstate differences within the context of the EARC. With the completion of the Tanzam railway, Tanzania was perceived by many to be reorienting its foreign policy toward the south, hoping to create stronger ties with Zambia and Mozambique at the expense of its involvement in the EAC. Other Community corporations faced similar funding problems and de facto decentralization appeared to be occurring in both the Harbours and Posts and Telecommunications corporations with separate operational centers for each established in Mombasa and Nairobi respectively.(53)

In June, 1975, Kenyan Attorney General Charles Njonjo urged his government to break up the EAC and create an independent railway system and customs administration. Nyerere had reportedly received similar advice from members of his political party and the Tanzanian cabinet. Although suggestions of EAC dissolution were strongly attacked in both the Kenyan Parliament and Tanzanian National Assembly, in October the Authority (still not meeting as a collective unit) finally agreed to an earlier Kenyan request for a thorough review of the Community's activities. William Demas, President of the Caribbean Development Bank, was chosen as Chairman of the review commission and given twelve months to prepare a report outlining necessary structural reforms. Like that headed by Philip in 1965, the Demas Commission was made up of ministers from each of three states, reflecting the obvious fact that the obstacles to East African coopera- tion were as much political as economic or institutional in nature.(54)

The Commission's task was complicated almost immediately by a sudden deterioration in relations between Kenya and Uganda. In February 1976, Amin announced that large sections of Kenya and the Sudan had been unjustly taken from Uganda during the period of British colonial rule. Vague pledges to ensure the "independence" of the region brought a swift response from Kenya. Kenyatta made clear his country's determination to defend its borders and placed a boycott on all Ugandan goods passing through Mombasa. Later, Kenya's western border was closed to road transport thus interrupting the flow of vital commodities to Uganda. Ugandan "clarifica- tions" which emphasized Amin's desire for friendly relations brought an end to the Kenyan restrictions in early March.(55)

What little hope remained for meaningful cooperation between the two states was further undermined on July 4 by Israel's use of the Nairobi airport for refueling on the re- turn flight from the dramatic rescue of Israeli hostages at Entebbe. Though Kenya denied any prearranged role in the operation, in response to accusations from Amin and the Ugandan press, a government statement denounced Amin as a "dictatorial fascist ruler." A bitter propaganda campaign followed and, on July 21, Kenya put into effect new currency regulations which effectively blocked trade between the two countries. Under severe economic pressure, Amin sent a dele- gation to Nairobi in early August. Agreement was reached on Kenyan terms resolving many of the immediate problems but the confrontation had an impact on Kenyan attitudes toward its East African partner. Editorialized the Daily Nation,

Our posture must be to diversify our exports

27

and imports to other areas and to find alternative routes so that economic blackmail
should never succeed...The fact that we were
blackmailed (militarily)...by Uganda in the
past few years, points to the need for a considerable defense capability...Given the ideological differences between us and our neighbours, there appear to be no good grounds for
expecting that things will get better in the
future.(56)

Prospects for the EAC clearly did not improve during
this period. In December, 1975, Nyerere spoke of the need for
"radical decentralization" of the common services(57) and in
April, 1976, the decision was made in Arusha to repatriate
all employees of the General Fund Services. Nyerere flew to
Nairobi in August following the thaw in Kenya's relations
with Uganda amid expectation of the long-awaited meeting of
the Authority. It did not materialize and the Demas report
appears to have offered little but a restatement of the divergent positions of the EAC members.(58)

With the failure to agree upon reform measures on either
the Authority or the Commission level, the process of disintegration accelerated. Ironically, the problems of East
African Airways, which had earlier been revived to become
perhaps the Community's most notable success, played a key
role in bringing on the EAC's final demise. Opposition to
Kenyan insistence on cutting back services on uneconomical
domestic routes had reportedly led Uganda and Tanzania to
withhold payment of funds destined for the EAAC's regional
headquarters in Nairobi. Short of operating funds, the EAAC
suspended most of its operations in January, 1977. Within
days, Kenya ordered the fleet grounded and announced the
formation of a national airline; Tanzania shortly formed its
own airline. Particularly angered by the timing of the
grounding order, which interfered with Tanzanian national
celebrations, Nyerere closed the border with Kenya on February 4 and seized vehicles with Kenyan registry. Kenya's profitable tourist trade from Nairobi to Tanzania's wildlife
parks was "permanently" banned shortly thereafter. The
break-up of the Railways and Harbours corporations followed.
A Kenyan railroad was formed in early February to replace the
EARC and in March Tanzania ordered the accounts of the EAHC

28

frozen. Unwanted foreign workers were dismissed by both countries from what had been Community positions in the EAHC and, by the end of the month, only the Posts and Telecommunications Corporation continued limited operations.(59)

Eleventh-hour efforts to preserve at least a skeletal Community structure were unsuccessful. Continued tension between Kenya and Tanzania over Nyerere's closure of the border and renewed Ugandan charges of Tanzanian plots against Amin made it difficult even to arrange a site for a meeting of the Finance Council. June ended with no agreement on the budget for the 1977-78 fiscal year and those services dependent upon the General Fund collapsed.(60)

With the disintegration of the EAC, the key remaining issue was how to divide the Community's assets and liabilities among its former members. In January 1978 Dr. Vider Umbricht, a Swiss banker and economist, was chosen as mediator to aid in this task. Vider's job was soon complicated by the military conflict between Amin and Tanzanian-backed Ugandan liberation forces. Amin's overthrow in 1979 and the partial thaw in Kenyan-Tanzanian relations which accompanied Daniel arap Moi's accession to the Kenyan presidency did rekindle hope for the revival of East African cooperation. Nyerere has been supportive, at least rhetorically, of such suggestions. Tanzania, however, has made clear the need to apportion the EAC's debts before any discussion can begin concerning the reopening of the Kenyan-Tanzanian border.(61) For the time being, the future of the integration process which the EAC was designed to further depends upon a successful resolution of the problems created by the Community's demise.

The chapters that follow explore in detail the reasons for the failure of the EAC to fulfill the ambitious goals of its founders. In Chapter III, John Ravenhill examines this issue in the context of theories of regional integration and offers observations concerning the general implications of the EAC experience for other less-developed countries.

Chapter II

Footnotes

1. Thomas M. Frank, _East African Unity Through Law_ (New Haven: Yale University Press, 1964), p. 9.

2. An excellent discussion of the consolidation of British control over East Africa is found in Frank, _East African Unity_, pp. 9-20.

3. Despatch from the Governor of Kenya to the Secretary of State for the Colonies, quoted in Frank, _East African Unity_, p. 31.

4. Frank, _East African Unity_, pp. 20-42. See also Peter Duignan, "Sir Robert Coryndon: A Model Governor," in eds. L.H. Gann and Peter Duignan, _African Proconsuls: European Governors in Africa_ (New York: The Free Press, 1978), pp. 343-346.

5. _Ibid._, pp. 42-54.

6. Jane Banfield, "The Structure and Administration of the East African Common Services Organization," in eds. C. Leys and P. Robson, _Federation in East Africa_ (Nairobi: Oxford University Press, 1965), p. 33.

7. A more complete analysis of the problem is found in Frank, _East African Unity_, pp. 44-51.

8. Banfield, "East African Common Services Organization," pp. 32-33.

9. The major self-contained services were the East African Railways and Harbours Administration and East African Posts and Telecommunications Administration, while the East African Airways Corporation later achieved a similar status.

10. Examples include a number of agricultural and medical research services, the East African Literature Bureau and the East African Income Tax Department.

11. A more detailed discussion of the accomplishments of this period is found in Frank, <u>East African Unity</u>, pp. 59-61.

12. <u>Ibid.</u>, pp. 63-70. See also selection by Hazlewood, below.

13. Walter Elkan and Leslie Nulty, "Economic Links in East Africa from 1945 to Independence," in eds., D.A. Low and Alison Smith, <u>History of East Africa</u> (3 vols., London: Oxford University Press, 1976), Vol. III, p. 343.

14. <u>Ibid.</u>, pp. 63-70.

15. For more discussion of the role of the Trusteeship Council during this period, see William Redman Duggan and John Civille, <u>Tanzania and Nyerere: A Study of Ujamaa and Nationhood</u> (Maryknoll, N.Y.: Orbis Books, 1976), pp. 24-41.

16. Frank, <u>East African Unity</u>, p. 72.

17. <u>Ibid.</u>, p. 83. A more detailed discussion of the structural changes made in creating the EACSO is found in Banfield, "East African Common Services Organization," pp. 34-38.

18. The Distributable Pool and the economic justifications for it is treated more fully in Arthur Hazlewood, <u>Economic Integration: The East African Experience</u> (New York: St. Martin's Press, 1975), pp. 39-45.

19. Frank, <u>East African Unity</u>, p. 93.

20. Uganda became independent in 1962, followed the next year by Kenya and Zanzibar, which merged with Tanganyika in 1964 to become the United Republic of Tanzania. (Note: For the sake of clarity, the name "Tanzania" will be used for the rest of the chapter even though, in several instances, it will refer to the period before the country was unified.)

21. "The Federation Declaration of 5th June, 1963," in eds. Leys and Robson, <u>Federation in East Africa</u>, pp. 205-208.

22. A more detailed discussion of the working party's negotiations is found in Frank, East African Unity, pp.
158-163. See also, "Federation Plan Stalls in East
Africa," Africa Report, Vol. 8, No. 9 (October 1963),
p. 20.

23. Hazlewood, Economic Integration, pp. 61-65.

24. Ibid., P. 56.

25. "The Kampala Agreement," East Africa Journal, Vol. 2,
No. 1. (April 1965), pp. 24-32. Further analysis of
the agreement is found in Hazlewood, Economic Integration, pp. 57-61. See also selection by Hazlewood,
below.

26. Domenico Mazzeo, "Problem of Regional Cooperation in
East Africa: Reasons and Consequences of the Collapse
of the East African Community," paper presented at the
annual convention of the International Studies Association, Toronto, March 21-24, 1979, p. 8.

27. Further discussion of the aftermath of the Kampala-
Mbale Agreements is found in Peter Robson, Economic Integration in Africa (Evanston, Illinois: Northwestern
University Press, 1968), pp. 151-153; Donald Rothchild,
"The Political Implications of the Treaty," East African Economic Review, Vol. 3, No. 3 (December 1967),
pp. 16-18; and Hazlewood, Economic Integration, pp.
64-68.

28. Treaty for East African Cooperation, signed at Kampala,
June 6, 1967, entered into force, December 1, 1967, in
International Legal Materials, Vol. 6 (1967), pp. 932-
1057.

29. Hazlewood, Economic Integration, p. 71.

30. The term "common market" is used throughout the Treaty
to denote what was, at best, a long term goal at the
time the Treaty was signed. Further analysis of the
Treaty's shortcomings in this respect is found in Y.P.
Ghai, "Legal Aspects of the Treaty for East African
Cooperation," East African Economic Review, Vol. 3,

No. 3 (December 1967), pp. 28-30.

31. Ibid., p. 28.

32. Treaty for East African Cooperation, Art. 2(1) (emphasis added).

33. Robson, Economic Integration in Africa, p. 157.

34. Treaty for East African Cooperation, Art. 20(3-4), p. 950.

35. Ibid., Art. 20 (6-8, 14-15), pp. 950-953.

36. Ibid., Annex VI, Art. 1(1) (b), p. 1003.

37. Ibid., Annex VI, Art. 13, p. 1010. Further analysis of the approach of the EADB is found in Hazlewood, Economic Integration, pp. 77-79.

38. Treaty for East African Cooperation, Art. 23, p. 956. See also Art. 19, p. 949.

39. For a table outlining the structure of the EAC see Ravenhill, below.

40. Ghai, "Legal Aspects," p. 31.

41. Ibid., pp. 33-34, 37.

42. Further analysis of the EAC structures is found in Ghai, "Legal Aspects," pp. 29-37.

43. An account of the early negotiations on association plans is found in Ingrid Doimi di Delupis, The East African Community and Common Market (London: Longman Group Ltd., 1970), pp. 125-128.

44. Julius Nyerere, statement of January 28, 1971, in African Research Bulletin, Vol. 8, No. 1 (February 1971), p. 1995.

45. Examples of the problems caused are found in Hazlewood, Economic Integration, pp. 89-90.

46. For a description of the dispute see "Peace Settlement," African Research Bulletin, Vol. 9, No. 10 (November 1972), p. 2626.

47. East African Standard, Oct. 9, 1972, in "Peace Settlement," p. 2627.

48. East African Standard, Feb. 7, 1973, in "Tension over Missing Kenyans," African Research Bulletin, Vol. 10, No. 2 (March 1973), p. 2751.

49. "Friendly Relations Restored," African Research Bulletin, Vol. 10, No. 5 (June 1973), p. 2853 and "Relations Fully Restored," African Research Bulletin, Vol. 10 No. 8 (September 1973), pp. 2949-2950.

50. A more complete analysis of the problems of the EAC through this period is found in Hazlewood, Economic Integration, pp. 88-145.

51. The problems of each of these corporations is analyzed further in Hazlewood, Economic Integration, pp. 96-104.

52. "East African Community: Threatened Split," African Research Bulletin, Vol. 11, No. 12 (January 1975), pp. 3450-3452; "East African Legislative Assembly: Meeting in Arusha," Africa Research Bulletin, Vol. 12, No. 1 (February 1975), p. 3485; and "Dispute Cools Down," African Research Bulletin, Vol. 12 No. 1 (February 1975), p. 3487.

53. "EAC: Progressive Deterioration of the Common Services," Keesing's Contemporary Archives (June 24, 1977), p. 28410; "East Africa: Future of the Community," Africa Confidential Vol. 16, No. 22 (November 7, 1975), pp. 3-5.

54. "Call for Dissolution," African Research Bulletin, Vol. 12, No. 6 (July 1975), p. 3649; "East Africa: Future of the Community," pp. 3-4.

55. "President Amin's Land Claims," Africa Research Bulletin, Vol. 13, No. 2 (March 1976), p. 3920.

56. <u>Daily Nation</u>, August 8, 1976, in "Moves to Improve Relations," <u>African Research Bulletin</u>, Vol. 13, No. 8 (September 1976), p. 4116.

57. "East African Community," <u>Africa Report</u>, Vol. 21, No. 1 (Jan.-Feb. 1976), p. 25.

58. "Workers to be Repatriated," <u>African Research Bulletin</u>, Vol. 13, No. 4 (May 1976), p. 3985; "Clampdown on Smuggling," <u>African Research Bulletin</u>, Vol. 13, No. 5 (June 1976), p. 4017; "Hate-Campaign Alleged," <u>African Research Bulletin</u>, Vol. 13, No. 4 (May 1976), pp. 3985-3986; "EAC" Progressive Disintegration of Common Services," <u>Kessing's Contemporary Archives</u> (June 24, 1977), p. 28410.

59. "East African Community," <u>Africa Report</u>, Vol. 22, No. 2 (March-April 1977), pp. 26-27; "EAC," <u>Africa Report</u>, Vol. 22, No. 3 (May-June 1977), pp. 26-27; "East Africa: Airline Gets Kiss of Life But...," <u>Africa Confidential</u>, Vol. 18, No. 2 (January 21, 1977), pp. 6-7; "EAC: Progressive Disintegration of Common Services," <u>Kessing's Contemporary Archives</u> (June 24, 1977), pp. 28411.

60. "East Africa in a Quagmire," <u>Africa Confidential</u>, Vol. 18, No. 13 (June 14, 1977), pp. 1-3; "EAC," <u>Africa Report</u>, Vol. 22, No. 5 (Sept.-Oct. 1977), p. 26.

61. "Moves to Normalize Relations," <u>African Research Bulletin</u> Vol. 13, No. 12 (January 1978), p. 4662-4663; "Border Cooperation," <u>African Research Bulletin</u>, Vol. 14, No. 1 (February 1978), p. 4701; Anthony J. Hughes, "Disunity in East Africa," <u>Africa Report</u>, Vol. 25, No. 6 (November-December 1979), pp. 4-10.

CHAPTER III

The Theory and Practice of Regional Integration in East Africa

John Ravenhill

"It is true we hear a lot about the problems of the East African Community. And indeed they do exist! It would be quite possible for some academic to write a book about them. But to what end? The thing about problems of international co-operation is that they get resolved if the will to co-operate is there. In East Africa I think we can claim that this will for united action does exist...."

Julius Nyerere "East African Co-operation is Alive", speech made in November 1970 reprinted in Nyerere Freedom and Development: Uhuru na Maendeleo (New York: Oxford University Press, 1973) p. 240.

Six years after Nyerere's speech the political will to sustain regional co-operation in East Africa had disappeared and the way was open for academics to write their books on the problems of the East African Community. The "end" for such analyses, which apparently eluded Nyerere in this speech, must be to provide a diagnosis of the failure of political will which explains, in less abstract terms than this somewhat mystical concept, the reasons which underlay changes in the partners' perceptions of the costs and benefits of continued regional co-operation. If this is to be something more than an academic exercise, the aim must be to discriminate between the idiosyncratic factors that precipitated the Community's collapse on the one hand, and the underlying problems (and the partners' attempts to deal with them) which tend to afflict all regional integration schemes among LDCs. Conclusions might then be drawn regarding the problems and prospects for such schemes in other areas.

Disintegration of the East African Community (EAC) is but the latest failure in a dismal record of regional co-operation attempts among LDCs. Although not unexpected, the demise of the EAC was particularly disappointing in that regional partnership in East Africa arguably was more extensive than that in any other such scheme in the world, given the existence of a common currency, common market, and fiscal harmonization between the three states. (Figure One charts the structure of the Community after the 1967 Treaty). But what must not be forgotten is that the regional arrangements were a colonial construction: in the post-independence

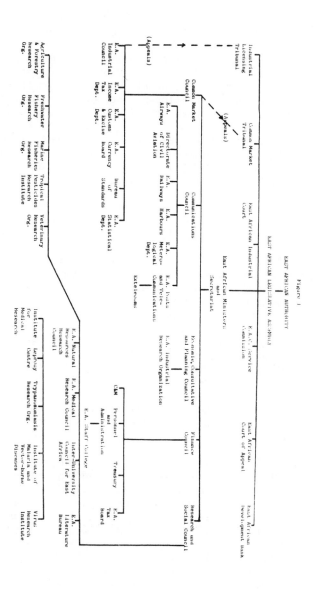

Figure 1

EAST AFRICAN AUTHORITY

period they were gradually but continually eroded.

Although regional co-operation in East Africa was of unusual scope, it was not matched by strong regional institutions. Under the colonial administration there had been no
concentration of decision-making power at the regional level.
Rather, the colonial civil service was a surrogate for a
regional authority, performing the task of conflict resolution and initiating new areas of regional co-operation. The
advent of independence led to a decentralization of these
powers and produced a vacuum at the regional level. Rothchild
has aptly characterized the impact of independence on East
African co-operation as a movement from "hegemony to bargaining": in the post-independence period disputes could be
settled and co-operative arrangements maintained only by bargaining among equals.(1)

Survival of the existing arrangements was now dependent
on the perceptions of the partner states regarding the con-
tribution that regional co-operation might make towards the
achievement of national development goals. As with other
customs areas among LDCs, the fundamental problem facing the
EAC was partner states' perceptions of the distribution of
gains from regional co-operation, the key factor in which the
location of industries established to serve the regional
market. It was widely held that operation of the common market in the colonial period had contributed to the disparity
in the rates of economic growth of the three partners. Viner,
for example, argued that the common external tariff had been
manipulated by colonial authorities in order to foster Kenyan
economic growth:

> The Tanganyika-Kenya Customs Union provides a
> striking instance where a territory was brought
> into a customs union by external authority in
> order to provide an expanded field for the
> tariff protection of the industries of another
> territory...The customs union operated to cre
> ate a protected market in Tanganyika for the
> produce of the small colony of British planters
> in Kenya, for whose welfare the British govern
> ment has shown a constant and marked solici
> tude.(2)

40

The colonial administration had maintained faith in a "trickle down" theory of economic growth--although it was admitted that Kenya had gained the largest share of benefits from integration, it was held that the prosperity of Kenya would have multiplier effects to the benefit of all partner states, and that there were net gains for all from both the common market and jointly-administered services.(3)

Following independence, maintenance of the regional scheme in its existing form was unacceptable for the two weaker states--Tanganyika and Uganda. The initial distributional crisis in the Community, immediately after the three states achieved their independence, may be perceived as an important turning point. For this offered an opportunity for the partners to reaffirm their commitment to a dynamic regional partnership--to engage in a process which Haas has termed the "upgrading of common interests" where the parties succeed in redefining their conflict so as to work out a solution at a higher level of integration, thereby providing task expansion for the regional institutions.(4)

The post-independence crisis illustrates a dilemma common to all regional groupings, namely that it is imperative to make continuous progress towards higher levels of integration if a dismantling of existing arrangements is to be avoided. Kitzinger made the suggestive analogy of a man riding a bicycle who must continue to pedal forward if he is not to fall off. Failure to maintain forward progress, to create additional benefits to be shared from new areas of co-operation, encourages the focusing of attention on the contentious issue of the distribution of existing gains from regional partnership. The extensiveness of regional arrangements in East Africa inherited at independence provided both opportunity and liability: opportunity in that it improved the prospects for reaching a "package deal" in which gains for one state in one area of co-operation, for example, the common market, might be offset by benefits for its partners elsewhere, e.g. the common services; a liability in that the constraints posed by existing arrangements on the member states' freedom of action in economic planning were intolerable for the states that perceived themselves as receiving an inadequate share of the benefits from regional co-operation. Major forward progress in joint policy-making in order to resolve the distributional problem was thus a prerequisite for

41

the maintenance of existing regional arrangements.

If the three states had realized their avowed intention to create an East African Federation, the necessary forward movement to sustain existing arrangements might have been achieved. Collapse of the precipitously contrived federations in West Africa and the West Indies, however, brings into question the ability of East Africa to have sustained political amalgamation--a conclusion which is reinforced by the partners' subsequent failure to sustain co-operation in the economic field. The post-independence history of East African co-operation has been the unsuccessful quest for an adequate solution to the distribution problem--unsuccessful in large part because of the unwillingness of the partner states to cede to a regional secretariat the powers necessary to enable planning of the location of industries dependent on the regional market.

The Kampala-Mbale Agreements represented the most promising attempt to resolve this problem: the subsequent failure to implement the Agreements testifies to the political sensitivity of the matter, and the low priority placed on regional co-operation by the Kenyan elite. It was not surprising therefore that the Treaty for East African Co-operation should not contain provisions for the regional allocation of industries. As Hazlewood has argued, the Treaty was the outcome of hard-fought inter-governmental negotiations and represented the maximum concessions that were politically feasible for the Kenyan government at the time.(5) But what is politically feasible is not necessarily sufficient for the task for which it is intended: the Treaty failed to tackle in an effective manner the most fundamental problems facing the Community.

Consequently it is difficult to accept Hazlewood's judgement that the instruments in the Treaty designed to effect a more equitable distribution of gains from regional co-operation were "appropriate to their purpose."(6) To evaluate this affirmation two inter-related criteria that he mentions in his chapter might be applied. The first, and most fundamental for the Community's survival, was whether the Treaty would reinforce members' perceptions that continued co-operation was worthwhile. The second was the stated objective of the Treaty to promote the "accelerated, harmonious and balanced development and sustained economic expansion of economic activities the benefits whereof shall be equitably shared." Hazlewood acknowledges that the Treaty manifestly failed on the first objective: what he fails to consider is the extent to which partners' perceptions were grounded in reality; that is, the failure of the Treaty's instruments to achieve the objective of a more balanced growth within the region.

A cursory examination of Table One demonstrates the lack of impact of the Treaty on the trade balance between Kenya and Tanzania.(7) Equally important are the data which illustrate the continuing predominance of Kenya in intra-Community exports of manufactured goods (Table Two)--a major factor in the favourable terms of trade enjoyed by Kenya in her commerce with her partners (Table Three), and in the positive balance of payments on intra-Community trade which helped offset Kenya's deficit in extra-Community transactions (Table Four). Further support for the idea that partners' perceptions of the costs and benefits of continued co-operation were not entirely illusory is found in Table Five which reveals the declining importance of intra-regional trade in the economies of the member states. In short, the regulatory devices established by the Treaty appear to have had no significant impact on the pattern of commerce of the Community in the nine years between its establishment and its demise.

It might be argued that nine years was an insufficient period for the effects of the measures to have been realized, and that in any case the Treaty's provisions were undermined by other policies pursued by the member states. To some extent there is truth in both arguments. But the Treaty's provisions were important in creating the psychological atmosphere in which further disintegrative measures were taken: there were few illusions at the time regarding the adequacy of the Treaty for solving the distributional problems. Such problems demanded solutions which would provide short-term results--if for no other reasons than the needs of political leaders to satisfy their domestic constituencies. Even if the Treaty had provided an effective long-term answer to the distribution problem, it would still have to be judged a failure since its inability to furnish means for an immediate amelioration of the problem was the cause of its inconsequential impact on partner states' perceptions.

43

While many other factors intervened to precipitate the collapse of the Community, the Treaty may be criticized for its failure to give regional co-operation in East Africa the institutional basis that would have restored it to the central position enjoyed during the colonial period. Of paramount importance was the distribution issue, for while this did not itself precipitate the collapse of the Community, the failure to effectively resolve this problem soured the atmosphere in which the Community operated and influenced in particular Tanzania's calculations of the balance sheet of potential gains and losses from co-operation. The principal regulatory device introduced by the Treaty--the transfer tax system--would seem a somewhat perverse method of attempting to equalize the benefits from regional co-operation for, in promoting this objective, the principle of the free movement of goods within the region was breached by the imposition of intra-Community tariffs.

Certainly the intention of the tax was not to encourage the inefficient duplication of industries within the region but there is little doubt that it had this effect. As Hazlewood acknowledges, the theoretical distinction between industries which might operate efficiently with a national market, and those which require the economies of scale provided by production for the regional market, breaks down in practice. Even if this had not been the case it is doubtful whether the transfer tax system would have provided a solution to the problem of imbalances in the location of those industries requiring the whole of the regional market for efficient operation, since there was nothing in the system to encourage such industries to locate in Uganda and Tanzania. The weaker states likely would have received only those industries able to operate efficiently in their domestic markets, i.e. those industries that they would have been able to attract regardless of whether or not they were members of a regional economic union. It was naive of the drafters of the Treaty to believe that rational economic calculations on the size of market necessary for efficient operation could be made in a vacuum, divorced from the politically-charged environment of disputes over the distribution of gains. Once deviation from the principle of the free movement of goods within the region was officially sanctioned, the system was open to all manner of abuse.

44

The transfer tax was the only instrument in the Treaty which directly addressed the central problem in the distribution question--the location of industry. The Treaty did contain other provisions relating to planning but these were ineffective. The Economic Consultative and Planning Council was charged with assisting the national planning of member states and with advising the Authority on the long-term planning of the common services. The Council's role was however merely consultative. Provision was also made for the continuation of the existing system of industrial licensing, established in 1948. However this system, which was much abused by the member states, was intended to ensure that there would be adequate supplies of inputs for industries seeking to locate in East Africa, and markets for their products, and was not concerned with the location of the industry within the region.(8)

Partner states increasingly perceived regional co-operation to be peripheral to the achievement of their national development goals and consequently were unwilling to place regional co-operation before the pursuit of short-term national interests. This trend was evident even before the three territories had achieved their independence, exemplified by the abolition of the East African Navy in 1961, and the similar fate of the East African Tourist Travel Association in 1963. A more serious reversal was the ending of the common currency following the collapse of the Kampala-Mbale Agreements. In 1965 Kenya passed a generous foreign investment protection law which infringed the principle of fiscal harmonization. By the time of the Treaty the three partners had already presided over a considerable dismantling of the co-operative arrangements inherited at independence. The Treaty did little to reverse this tendency--after 1967 the common market was a fiction; the Treaty made no provision for the free movement of labour or capital within the region. The introduction and differential application of sales taxes in the three states undermined the principle of a common external tariff, harmonization of income tax systems effectively ended in 1972. Non-tariff barriers to economic co-operation multiplied: of particular importance were state trading corporations which, through a variety of means, interfered with the freedom of intra-regional trade.(9)

The Treaty for East African Co-operation incorporated

45

the maximum concessions that could be extracted from the partner states at the time given the bounds of political feasibility. Yet the Treaty clearly failed to provide mechanisms to sustain even the existing scope of regional co-operation among LDC's has been so dismal. To understand this, it is necessary to probe the structural factors that provide the economic and political backcloth to such integration schemes.

The Economic and Political Background(10)

Dissolution of the East African Community was disappointing in view not only of the sophisticated scope of regional activities inherited at independence but also in that the political and economic background factors within the region were generally judged to be more favourable for the support of regional co-operation than those prevailing in other Third-world regional groupings.(11) In the light of the East African experience, the viability of regional co-operation as a development strategy for LDC's is called into question.

Benefits from the creation of free trade areas arise only where tariffs have been a major impediment to inter-territorial trade. Among most LDC's, and in Africa in particular, this is rarely the case. The problem is not so much a matter of tariff barriers but of the inability of states to produce the goods which satisfy the import needs of their neighbours. This is reflected in the low percentage of African states' external transactions that are accounted for by intra-Continental trade (although again this was a dimension on which the EAC was unusually favoured). In this milieu, the creation of customs unions enjoys little legitimacy under neo-classical theory which judges their merit according to the benefits derived from trade creation.

Customs unions among LDC's are designed instead to be instruments of trade diversion in which the erection of a common external tariff facilitates import substitution on a regional scale, bringing into employment otherwise idle factors of production. An enlarged regional market is expected to attract additional inputs especially foreign capital, and enable the realization of economies of scale.

But where regional co-operation is justified primarily by reference to its ability to attract import-substituting industries, the question of the location of these industries within the region immediately comes to the fore.

Given the extreme poverty of most African economies, reflected in low levels of industrialization and high rates of unemployment, the establishment of a single new industry within a country can have a major economic impact and is consequently a matter of great political sensitivity. The tendency of customs unions to lead to a skewed distribution of benefits as "backwash" effects predominate over "spread" effects is well-documented. Growth occurs primarily in those areas which have enjoyed an initial advantage. Economic co-operation among LDC's is unlikely to be sustained unless all partners make net gains and these gains are perceived to be shared relatively equitably. For this to occur, the "natural" economic tendency towards unequal development must be counteracted by political measures. Multiplier effects produced by the establishment of new industries make the question of industrial location the most contentious of distributional issues. For the weaker partners there is little benefit to be gained from exchanging an extra-regional supplier for one within a neighbouring state, particularly since the latter may well produce at higher cost, being protected from competition by the common external tariff.

Fiscal transfers from more fortunate to the less prosperous members of a regional scheme are in themselves an insufficient solution to the distribution problem. Such transfers may amount to little more than the customs revenue foregone as a result of the exclusion of extra-regional imports(12), and are an inadequate substitute for the employment opportunities and such spinoffs as improved local skills, technology and infrastructure—not to forget prestige—which are brought by industrial development. Manipulation of rates of taxation to encourage substitution of local production for imports from more developed states within a region has the effect—regardless of whether this was the intention—of encouraging the duplication of inefficient plants within a region. Frequently the primary beneficiaries of such policies are multinational corporations, able to establish uneconomic plant which is protected from competition from within the region by the tax system, and from extra-regional rivals by the external tariff. One of the principal justifications for the creation of customs unions-- the realization of economies of scale in producing for a larger market--is also undermined.

Regional industrial planning would appear to offer the only satisfactory long-term solution to the distribution crisis that plagues third-world integrative schemes. Yet this again raises the problem of the disjunction between political necessity and political feasibility. Planning on a regional scale would necessitate a transfer of sovereignty to regional institutions that few third world governments would be willing to endorse. This is more than a matter of the disinclination of African governments to part with their newly-won sovereignty: although this factor certainly is of some consequence, the similar problems encountered in Latin America, where states in many cases have enjoyed political sovereignty for longer than some of the member countries of the European Community, suggest that more fundamental influences are operative.

The inter-relationship between economic and political factors is immediately apparent. One factor which has already been noted is the importance that of necessity is attached to industrialization. Even for political leaders in the relatively prosperous states in a regional partnership, it is politically unfeasible to be seen to be sacrificing domestic economic growth for the sake of regional partnership unless offsetting benefits can be realized in the short-term from the latter. Low level of economic development also precludes the emergence of interest groups which were perceived by neofunctionalist theorists as providing a major impetus in a movement towards further integration. A major problem faced by third world integrative schemes is in fact the absence of a domestic constituency. For political leaders there are few rewards in the short-run to be won at the regional level. For civil servants, bureaucratic self-interest tends against any support for an extension of regional authority which might encroach on their own. Even the commitment of business interests to closer regional co-operation is unsure--particularly if this involves the allocation of industries which might otherwise have been established locally to the weaker partner states.

Perceptions of the benefits to be derived from closer regional partnership are coloured also by the apparent attractiveness of alternative opportunities. A further characteristic of Third World economies is important in this instance--their asymmetrical interdependence with the developed world. African states compete not only in their role as suppliers of raw materials and agricultural products in the international division of labour but also in their efforts to attract foreign investment, skills and technology. A close relationship with foreign partners able to supply these developmental prerequisites may be perceived as more attractive, if a choice has to be made, than an emphasis on continued co-operation with neighbours who are equally impoverished. This is particularly the case if manufacturing for export to Western markets, via the medium of multinational corporations, appears feasible. Again the key factor here is the perception of opportunities, regardless of whether they are adequately grounded in economic reality. If the price of continued regional co-operation is industrial planning, why run the risk of alienating foreign investors when manufacturing for export appears to hold forth prospects for more rapid growth than manufacturing for import-substitution, especially when the benefits of the latter have to be shared with weaker partners?

A further consequence of the weakness and asymmetrical interdependence that is characteristic of African economies is the major disruptive effect that environmental and external influences can have on economic growth. Nowhere is this more evident than in the impact of oil price rises on African economies. Whether balance of payments crises are caused by external influences as in this case, or by environmental factors such as drought which leads to failure of a major export crop, it is unlikely that their effects will be confined to the domestic economy. In the search for saving in foreign exchange, transactions with regional partners will also be curtailed. This might not necessarily have a major disruptive effect if consultations are engaged in--however where the climate of regional co-operation is already sour, unilateral action can serve as a precipitant of total collapse. The mechanisms provided in the EAC for the settlement of intraregional payments imbalances ensured that regional transactions would not be unaffcted when foreign exchange problems arose for the member states. A ceiling of

Shs. 10 millions placed on the annual payments deficits with regional partners (including trade, travel, investment income, capital flows and community corporation funds transfers) that could be met with local currency made these imbalances particularly burdensome for Tanzania and Uganda. Local currency financed only 5% of Tanzania's and 4% of Uganda's annual deficits with Kenya. Efforts to conserve scarce foreign exchange by delaying transfers of revenue to community corporation headquarters were to be a major precipitating factor in the Community's collapse. This again provides an instance where the drafters of the Treaty appear to have lacked foresight.

Domestic political turbulence and the forcible overthrow of regimes frequently have provided the precipitants which have ended regional co-operative projects. Here it is necessary to distinguish between the idiosyncracies of a particular case, e.g. Amin's impact on the EAC, and the potential that exists in all systems of personalized rule for instability in domestic politics, which can spill-over to disrupt relationships in the regional area. The unwillingness of African states to cede any significant power to regional secretariants has most often resulted in an arrangement, as was the case with the EAC, where heads of state of member countries are the supreme decision-making authority. Smooth functioning of the co-operative arrangements is wholly dependent on the maintenance of cordial relationships between the personalities concerned: there is no insulation of regional co-operation from the instabilities of domestic politics and contentious inter-state disputes. Greater autonomy for regional institutions might facilitate the maintenance of a positive political commitment on the part of member states by providing an arena in which conflicts may be resolved before they become enveloped in emotional debate in national political circles. But economic and political structural factors are unpropitious for the development of strong regional secretariats: a lack of institutionalization of regional partnership is the concomitant of the lack of institutionalization of government in the member states.

Finally, mention must be made of the effect that the holding of incongruous ideologies by regional partners can have on co-operative ventures. Divergence in development strategies can impair efforts to engineer an equitable dis-

50

tribution of gains from regional co-operation in that, for example, member states pursue divergent policies towards foreign investment. In the East African case, Kenya's initial advantage resulting from privileged treatment during the colonial period and her favourable geographical position, were reinforced by the generous treatment afforded foreign capital. Although Tanzania has never ruled out the participation of foreign private investment in her development plans, government policies which aimed at strictly prescribing the conditions on which foreign capital was acceptable served to create an atmosphere of uncertainty. Consequently it was unsurprising that foreign investors attempted to service the regional market as much as possible from plants established in Kenya. For Kenyan politicians, this was a vindication of their strategy--as far as they were concerned the imbalances in benefits from regional co-operation were the result of the inadequacies of the development policies pursued by her partners. Ideological differences tend to intensify competition between partner states and harden attitudes against compromise. Kenya's commitment to a development path founded on the co-operation of local and external private capital ruled out the possibility of agreement to industrial planning on a regional scale.

Hazlewood might be correct in arguing that it is a "conclusion of despair that mutually benefiticial economic co-operation requires a close similarity of social and political outlook."(13) Nevertheless, the record of integrative attempts among LDC's provides little reason for optimism. It would be more useful to attempt to differentiate between types of economic co-operation according to the impact that ideological divergence between the partners has on their prospects. For limited functional projects, e.g. joint construction of a dam, there is no logical reason why potential partners with markedly different ideologies should not engage in a successful joint endeavour--although this has not prevented inter-state disputes from disrupting such ventures in West Africa, e.g. the Organization of Senegal River States. For more ambitious schemes such as customs unions, formidable difficulties can be presented by ideological divergence, especially with regard to attitudes towards foreign investment, which preclude a satisfactory solution of the distribution issue. This is not to argue that a regional partnership between states with compatible ideologies will necessarily succeed. Such are the constraints that are imposed by the economic environment, and nationalist sentiments in LDC's are so strong, that even a union among states with a strong commitment to regional co-operation may founder on the distributional problem. Dependency theorists who perceive regional self-reliance as a viable counter-dependency option for LDC's have underestimated the propensity of nationalism to overcome the most sincere of commitments to socialist internationalism.

Conclusion

For many students of regional integration the demise of the East African Community was a question not of "if" but "when". The matter of "how" was also of some interest in that there appeared to be a hope of saving some of the jointly-administered services even if the common market was to disappear. This was not to be the case as a result of the bitterness of the circumstances in which dissolution occurred. The failure of regional co-operation in East Africa confirmed predictions of integration theorists regarding the difficulties of sustaining Third World integrative schemes owing to the unfavourable economic and political background. If demise of the Community appeared inevitable, it is perhaps unfair to place a heavy burden of blame for its failure on the provisions of the 1967 Treaty: certainly the background political factors were such as to rule the necessary measures to be politically unfeasible.

Nevertheless, unless one is to accept an argument which perceives the economic and political factors as completely deterministic, and successful regional co-operation among LDC's as a lost cause, some blame for the Community's demise must be attributed to the inadequacies of the Treaty, in particular the instruments whose purpose was the attainment of a more equitable distribution of benefits from regional partnership. Rather than laying the foundation for future forward movement of the Community, the Treaty provided for a further abandonment of the fundamental principles on which co-operation had been based. None of the measures in the Treaty was capable of providing--nor, indeed, was intended to seek--a solution to the problem of the location of industries whose efficient operation was dependent on the re-

52

alization of economies of scale brought about by production for the regional market. Neither were the regulatory instruments capable of effecting a substantial equalization of benefits in the short-to-medium terms--the time period in which the effectiveness of the Treaty inevitably was judged.

Dissolution of the Community raises theoretical issues regarding the feasibility of integrative schemes among LDC's --at least with respect to the form in which they have often been expressed, namely customs unions. Students of regional integration have amply documented the tendency towards an uneven distribution of benefits from customs unions, and the disruptive effect that this has on integrative schemes.(14) Planning of industrial location appears to offer the only long-term solution to this problem, necessitating the transfer of decision-making power to a regional secretariat. This is also the case if the scheme has counter-dependency ambitions, i.e. if the partner states seek to use the bargaining power that they can exert through joint action vis-a-vis purchasers for their primary products, or investors seeking to locate within the region.(15) But the strength of national jealousies is such that even where an unusual degree of decision-making autonomy is granted to a regional organ, member governments may undermine the authority of the secretariat by refusing to implement decisions made at the regional level. This would appear to have been the fate of the Andean Pact.(16)

Again, the unhappy conclusion is that unfavourable political and economic structural factors eventually subvert the arrangements of even the best-planned Third World integrative schemes. The current evolution of the world economy towards an internationalization of manufacturing production is an inducement for LDC's to seek closer economic co-operation with industrialized states rather than with their neighbours. With growing concern in the West regarding the security of supply of raw materials, the incentives offered to LDC's to move in this direction will probably strengthen. The political vision and economic capacity necessary for states to be able and willing to make sacrifices of national gains for the sake of regional co-operation perhaps requires the emergence of more developed economies, the existence of groups with material or bureaucratic interests in the furthering of regional integration, and/or the emergency of regional powers

able to make the necessary side-payments to weaker partners
to maintain their interest in the scheme. Venezuela appears
to be assuming this role in the Andean Pact. It was the mis-
fortune of the Community that no partner had the resources or
political will to perform a similar task for East Africa.

Footnotes

1. Donald Rothchild, "From Hegemony to Bargaining in East African Relations," Journal of African Studies 1, 4 (Winter 1974) pp. 390-416.

2. Jacob Viner, The Customs Union Issue (London: Stevens & Sons, 1950) p. 70. This sentiment is echoed by T. A. Kennedy "The East African Customs Union: Some Features of Its History and Operation," in Donald Rothchild (ed.) Politics of Integration: An East African Documentary (Nairobi: East African Publishing House, 1968) pp. 169-173.

3. The Raisman Commission noted that there had been a "great disparity" between the growth rates of the separate territories but concluded nevertheless that "it is very doubtful whether Uganda or Tanganyika could be setting up barriers within the common market have gained more than they would have lost by the certain impoverishment of East Africa as a whole." Excerpts from the Raisman Report in Ibid., pp. 187-8.

4. Ernst B. Haas, "International Integration: The European and the Universal Process" in Michael Hodges (ed.) European Integration (Harmondsworth: Penguin, 1972) pp. 93-6.

5. See Chapter V of this volume; also Hazlewood Economic Integration: The East African Experience (London: Heinemann, 1975) passim.

6. See Hazlewood below, P. 128.

7. Although not entirely satisfactory as a measure of the distribution of benefits and costs from regional cooperation (since all of the trade between the partners is not dependent onthe external tariff, and no consideration is given to such potential compensating factors as cross-subsidization of services), the balance of trade is the most convenient and widely used indicator. A useful discussion of the problems involved in

the measurement of the effects of integration is found in UNCTAD <u>Current Problems of Economic Integration</u> [TD/B/394] (Geneva: 1973).

8. Yash P. Ghai, "East African Industrial Licensing Scheme: A Device for the Regional Allocation of Industry," <u>Journal of Common Market Studies</u> XII, 3 (1974) pp. 265-295. See also East African Community, <u>Review of Economic Integration Activities within the East African Community 1973-74</u> (Arusha: Common Market and Economic Affairs Secretariat, May 1974) p. 164.

9. Article 16 of the Treaty for East African Co-operation stated that the Partner States "recognize" that one-channel marketing was incompatible with the Treaty to the extent that it frustrated the benefits of free trade but did not specify what actions or sanctions might be taken if a breach of this type occurred. A useful discussion of the effects of state trading is found in Dharam P. Ghai "State Trading and Regional Economic Integration: The East African Experience," <u>Journal of Common Market Studies</u> XII, 3 (1974) pp. 296-318.

10. This section draws on the author's "Regional Integration and Development in Africa: Lessons from the East African Community," <u>Journal of Commonwealth and Comparative Politics</u> (November 1979), London: Frank Cass & Co.

11. Neo-functionalist integration theorists proposed the following variables as indicators of the likely success of integrative schemes (the evaluations for East Africa made by Nye are in parentheses): (A) Background Conditions: size of units (mixed-); rate of transaction (Mixed+); pluralism--modern (low); elite complementarity (high-0. (B) Process conditions: Decision-making style (mixed); rate of transaction (mixed+); adaptability of governments (mixed). Ernst B. Haas & Philippe C. Schmitter "Economics and Differential Patterns of Political Integration: Projects about Unity in Latin America," in <u>International Political Communities</u> (New York: Doubleday, 1966); Joseph S. Nye "Patterns and Catalysts in Regional Integration," <u>International Organization</u> XIX (August 1965) pp. 870-84. See also

56

Nye <u>Peace in Parts</u> (Boston: Little Brown, 1971); and Nye, "Comparing Common Markets: A Revised Neo-Functionalist Model," in Leon N. Lindberg & Stuart A. Scheingold (Eds.) <u>Regional Integration: Theory and Research</u> (Cambridge: Harvard University Press, 1971) pp. 192-231.

12. Domenico Mazzeo quotes the following figures for fiscal transfers made under the Distributable Pool proposed by the Raisman Commission, for the year 1962-3: £ 312,000 to Tanganyika £ 288,000 to Uganda. "Problems of Regional Co-operation in East Africa: Reasons and Consequences of the Collapse of the East African Community," p. 6. Paper presented to the annual convention of the International Studies Association, Toronto, March 21-24, 1979. In the period 1968-72 Tanzania received an average Shs. 48 millions per year in revenue from transfer taxes imposed on approximately 20% of manufactured imports from Kenya.

13. See Hazlewood below, p. 135.

14. B. Balassa <u>The Theory of Economic Integration</u> (Homewood, Ill.: 1961); Lynn K. Mytelka "The Salience of Gains in Third-World Integrative Systems," <u>World Politics</u> XXV, 2 (January 1973) pp. 236-250.

15. W. Andrew Axline, "Underdevelopment, Dependence and Integration: The Politics of Regionalism in the Third World," <u>International Organization</u> 31, 1 (Winter 1977) pp. 83-105.

16. Rafael Vargas-Hidalgo, "The Crisis of the Andean Pact: Lessons for Integration among Developing Countries," <u>Journal of Common Market Studies</u> XVII, 3 (March 1979) pp. 213-226.

APPENDIX

Table 1: Inter-Territorial Trade 1964-1975 (Sh. millions)

(A) KENYA

Year	To U	From U	K/U Balance	To T	From T	K/T Balance	To U&T	From U&T	K/U&T Balance
1964	252	145	+107	266	82	+184	518	227	+291
1965	307	143	+164	282	91	+190	589	234	+354
1966	337	146	+190	266	76	+190	602	222	+380
1967	296	203	+ 93	228	66	+162	524	269	+254
1968	265	174	+ 92	261	74	+188	529	247	+280
1969	319	156	+163	257	80	+177	576	236	+340
1970	334	201	+133	295	119	+176	629	320	+309
1971	383	161	+222	295	159	+136	678	319	+359
1972	330	152	+178	326	118	+208	666	269	+386
1973	438	93	+345	337	153	+184	775	246	+529
1974	586	75	+510	381	191	+190	996	266	+730
1975	517	29	+488	406	169	+237	923	198	+725
1976	537	15	+522	459	232	+227	996	247	+749

(B) UGANDA

Year	To K	From K	U/K Balance	To T	From T	U/T Balance	To K&T	From K&T	U/K&T Balance
1964	145	252	-107	49	20	+ 28	193	272	- 79
1965	143	307	-164	52	27	+ 25	195	334	-139
1966	146	337	-190	64	17	+ 46	209	354	-145
1967	203	296	- 93	49	15	+ 34	252	311	- 59
1968	174	265	- 92	41	17	+ 23	214	282	- 69
1969	156	319	-163	34	24	+ 10	190	343	-152
1970	201	334	-133	40	29	+ 11	241	363	-122
1971	161	383	-222	16	38	- 22	177	421	-244
1972	152	330	-178	6	15	- 10	157	346	-189
1973	93	438	-345	2	18	- 16	95	456	-361
1974	75	586	-511	–	26	- 26	75	612	-536
1975	29	517	-488	–	6	- 6	29	523	-494
1976	15	537	-522	–	6	- 6	15	543	-528

Table 1 (continued)

(C) TANZANIA

Year	To K	From K	T/K Balance	To U	From U	T/U Balance	To K&U	From K&U	T/K&U Balance
1964	82	266	-184	20	48	- 28	103	318	-215
1965	91	282	-190	27	52	- 25	118	334	-215
1966	76	266	-190	17	62	- 46	93	328	-235
1967	66	228	-162	15	49	- 34	81	276	-196
1968	74	261	-188	17	41	- 23	91	302	-211
1969	80	257	-177	24	34	- 10	104	291	-187
1970	119	295	-176	29	40	- 11	148	335	-187
1971	159	295	-136	38	16	+ 22	197	311	-155
1972	118	326	-208	15	6	+ 10	133	332	-198
1973	153	337	-184	18	2	+ 16	171	339	-168
1974	191	381	-190	26	-	+ 26	217	381	-164
1975	169	406	-237	6	-	+ 6	174	406	-232
1976	232	459	-227	6	-	+ 6	238	459	-221

Source: For 1964-73, E.A.C., Review of Economic Interaction
Activities in the East African Community 1973-74,(Arusha:
Common Market and Economic Affairs Secretariat, May,
1974). For 1974 and 1975, Africa Research Bulletin:
Economic, Financial and Technical Series 13 (3) April 30,
1976, p. 3831.

Table 2: Percentage of Inter-Territorial Exports that Are Manufactured Goods

	1971	1972	1973	1974	1975
KENYA	87.0	84.4	82.9	83.0	89.6
TANZANIA	68.6	57.9	67.5	58.1	61.1
UGANDA	84.9	76.8	74.0	48.7	41.0

Source: Kenya, Economic Survey, 1976

Table 3: Kenya's Terms of Trade (1964 = 100)

	1968	1969	1970	1971	1972	1973	1974
External trade	90	90	97	85	84	85	68
Inter-Territorial trade	105	102	102	112	106	111	109
Total	96	94	99	93	94	92	75

Source: Kenya, Economic Survey, 1976

Table 4: Kenya's Balance of Trade (K£ millions)

	1971	1972	1973	1974	1975
Outside East Africa	-105.7	-82.2	-76.9	-182.9	-161.1
With Uganda and Tanzania	17.9	19.3	26.5	35.0	36.3
Total	- 87.8	-62.9	-50.4	-147.9	-124.8

Source: Kenya, Economic Survey, 1976

Table 5: Inter-Territorial Trade as Percentage of Total Trade

(A) Inter-Territorial Imports as a Percentage of Total Imports

	1971	1972	1973	1974	1975	1976
Kenya	7.9	7.1	5.6	5.0	2.8	3.0
Tanzania	11.4	11.3	9.7	6.6	7.1	8.8
Uganda	23.6	29.8	40.0	39.3	35.6	45.4

(B) Inter-Territorial Exports as a Percentage of Total Exports

	1971	1972	1973	1974	1975	1976
Kenya	30.2	25.6	23.1	22.1	20.8	15.7
Tanzania	9.9	5.8	6.6	7.3	6.3	5.9
Uganda	9.5	7.8	4.3	3.2	1.5	0.5

Source: Calculated from data in EAC Statistical Department, Economic and Statistical Review Quarterly and East African Customs and Excise Department, Annual Trade Reports.

CHAPTER IV

Who Killed the East African Community?

Richard Fredland

Who Killed the East African Community?(1)

After a period of predictions regarding its demise extending over fully half its short lifetime, the East African Community finally succumbed in mid-1977. Hailed by many and representing the high hopes of many more as one strategem by which developing countries could better their lot vis-a-vis the rich countries at relatively little cost, the Community with its variety of corporations(2) and service organizations(3) struggled for ten years to an ignominious end-- eaten away finally by petty political concerns compounded by major economic impediments.

While the recency of the issue makes it very sensitive politically, it is still possible as well as politically interesting to inquire into the causes of its failure, while recognizing that a more detached view at some future time might yield a different analysis. A variety of hypotheses have appeared. Most of these surfaced in one form or another as criticisms of the Community during its active lifetime. This article presents a collection of these speculative causes of the Community's demise and assesses the role each played in that demise. Finally, on the basis of recent field research in Kenya, we will explore the future role there might be for regional association in East Africa.

* * *

Probably the most widespread diagnosis of the ailment of the Community during its last year was the divergent paths Kenya and Tanzania have been taking, most specifically economically. With much the effect of compound interest, Kenya has become increasingly capitalist with an economy thoroughly infused with Western capital and technology with the attendant external control and influence. Tanzania, on the other hand, has increasingly pursued the path of self-directed socialist development as articulated by its President Nyerere.(4) Uganda is frequently included in this particular diagnosis on the socialist side of the divergence even though no overall plan or ideology was discernible in Idi Amin's bloody fiefdom. State corporations expanded both under the Obote and Amin regimes in Uganda and controlled a significant portion of what remained of the economy. Even six months after Amin's overthrow by Tanzanian forces coupled with Ugandan exiles the political and economic infrastructure in Uganda remained a shambles--a measure of the completeness of Uganda's destruction under Amin's stewardship. And while Kenya, however, does maintain several state corporations, e.g., Kenya Cooperative Creameries, they are the exception to both the practical as well as the ideological rule. Because Tanzania has vigorously pursued its formulated development programs which have caused significant social as well as economic disruption in vivid contrast to Kenya's ostensible political, social, and economic stability, stresses have been magnified.

Especially for ideologues it is convenient to attribute this substantial stress as the cause of failure. And for Kenyan sympathizers this is given added credence by the fact that Tanzanian President Nyerere, who became Chairman of the East African Authority in 1970, refused to summon a meeting of that body because of his unwillingness to sit at the same table with Ugandan President Amin. Kenya, on the other hand, expressed repeatedly a willingness to meet with Uganda in the interest of the Community. This can hardly be ascribed as the cause of the Community collapse though symptomatically it was important in diagnosing the illness. Even President Nyerere's detractors concede that he is a man of principle, and so far as this observer is aware no responsible analyst has placed the "smoking gun" in his hand. Had the Authority met, the rancor that was likely to have spilled onto the table would likely have made the absence of a meeting a greater contributor to the survival of the Community than the prescribed meeting itself.

Another prime source of strains in the Community--one which has plagued it since before its inception--is the unequal levels of development among the three members.(5) While this has many dimensions, one illustration serves to demonstrate the deep-seated nature of the development gap(6) between Kenya and her two partners. One of the two surviving East African Community institutions is the East African Development Bank,(7) a separately-governed, independently-financed corporation. The charter of the Bank, taking cognizance of the uneven development of the three states, provided for equal participation by the three states,(8) but the Bank's development activity was to be distributed distinctly

65

unevenly for the ostensible purpose of evening economic developments: 38.75% in Tanzania, 38.75% in Uganda, but only 22.5% in Kenya. While on the surface this would suggest a considerable advantage to Tanzania and Urganda, in reality Kenya continued to surge ahead in capital investment because (a) it was building on a much stronger, long-established base, (b) its stable capitalist system allowed it to generate external funds, particularly from the West, independently of the community, and (c) Bank assets were very modest: $20,000,000. Throughout the life of the Community, as well as before, Kenya dominated economic activity in East Africa, especially in terms of development potential. In the brief compass of this paper it is not possible to explore all the dimensions of economic disparity between Kenya and its two partners. A perusal of the Economic and Statistical Review, issued periodically by the East African Statistical Department, will illustrate many of the dimensions of this gap.

An example of how fragile Community cooperation was centered around the tourist trade--both on economic and philosophical levels. Tanzania had sought to counter Kenya's exploitation of the tourist trade in the early 1970's by constructing the Kilimanjaro International Airport within sight of the fabled peak and a short drive from Arusha, the usual jumping-off point for tours to Tanzania's game areas. But because of an absence of international-standard services (incoming passengers sometimes found no customs officials and no ground transportation, for example) Kilimanjaro did not flourish. Also ideology intruded again: Tanzania had opposed the bourgeois intrusion of tourists' values and decadence, a concern increasingly being voiced in Kenya, as well. The economic facts of tourist spending: that it does not spready very widely through the society, that it fosters production of developmentally-irrelevant luxury facilities and goods, that it supports such socially undesirable activities as gambling, prostitution, and alcohol consumption all contributed to the widespread disenchantment and explain socialist Tanzania's attitude. The economic development attributable to tourism is of little value to an emerging economy. Few Tanzanians require luxury hotels, bars, or brothels. The purported "trickle down" of income of Tanzanians employed in or supplying these activities is not seen as adequately redeeming. The result has been continued Kenyan development of her tourist activities while Tanzania's game lodges stood largely vacant.

Kenya's central geographic position further enhanced her advantage. As is discussed regarding the railways below, Kenya benefitted by trade passing through to both Tanzania and Uganda as well as elsewhere. This rendered Nairobi a logical center of economic as well as other infrastructure activity, so that an uncommon proportion of joint activity was centered there, especially in earlier days. This was enhanced by Nairobi's becoming upon independence the international center for Eastern Africa, for example as the only developing country hosting a UN specialized agency, the UN Environment Program. Logically, Nairobi was the manufacturing, distribution, cultural, and financial center for East Africa as well.

A digression into integration theory elaborates the entire system of analysis at this point: Politically, it must be assumed that in any integration effort the participants will distinctly perceive themselves receiving benefits which exceed the cost of participation. In effect the sum should be theoretically, as well as actually, greater than its respective parts. The more open the political system, the more apparent this must be so that requisite political support can be mustered and maintained. In East Africa, Kenya would have to be ranked as most open politically with Tanzania in the middle. Under Amin Uganda would have been off any reasonable scale. Applying that concept to Kenya's willingness to benefit unequally in the Bank's activity, for example, Kenya was trading off a slight cost there for the considerable advantage of having virtually unfettered access to the Tanzanian and Ugandan markets for her relatively sophisticated exports as well as serving as the financial center for the region.

Given the poverty of Tanzania, Kenya's progress created a visible development gap that was politically intolerable, and which finally resulted in a closing of the border between the two states in early 1977. There is a proximate, symptomatic cause of the border closing which resulted from the Kenyan's aggressively and successfully seeking tourists in Europe, North America, and Japan. The typical tourist flew into Nairobi's international airport via East African

67

(now Kenyan) Airways, lodged at a Nairobi hotel (reputedly owned at least in part by one or another member of President Kenyatta's Cabinet), hired a van owned by a Nairobi-based touring company (though perhaps controlled by a British parent corporation), and drove or was chauffeured to Tanzania for two or three days of game viewing in a Tanzanian national park. Tanzania's Serengeti and Manyara National Parks--the former encompassing the incomparable Ngorongoro Crater--are the pre-eminent game preserves in East Africa. Consequently, of perhaps US $2200 paid by the tourist, as little as $200 was earned by Tanzania while the remainder, excluding air fare, was earned by--or at least in--Kenya.

There was another dimension to the Kenya-Tanzania strain which was much more fundamental, and ideological. In recent years President Nyerere's program of establishing Ujamaa communal villages in Tanzania as a keystone to his overall development strategy has come upon hard times. The incentives offered rural villagers to join Ujamaa villages--a new school, a well, a clinic--demanded far greater resources than the Tanzanian government could provide, and so the process tended to degenerate into instances of Tanzanian soldiers forcing villagers at gunpoint into newly-established Ujamaa villages--still without the promised incentives being available. As economic strains mounted in Tanzania, the economy faltered, further exaggerating the already-considerable and very visible differences in levels of apparent development between the two neighbors. Thus the border closing made political sense as a means of terminating Kenya's exploitation of the Tanzanian market as well as a means of insulating Tanzania's populace from the relative prosperity in Kenya which resulted in smuggling of currency, coffee, and other scarce consumer items.

Operation of two Community corporations also specifically contributed to grief. Aside from periodic charges of poor management and corruption, especially regarding the railways, both the airways and railways were beset by deep-seated differences of opinion between Kenya and Tanzania as to objectives.

Kenya is a more compact country with a more sophisticated transportation infrastructure than Tanzania. Tanzania's policy of rural development, coupled with her inferior transportation systems and resources, resulted in wide dispersal of her population. Consequently, Tanzania determined that East African Airways should serve primarily as a domestic carrier and communication medium. Kenya, on the other hand, saw the airline as an international carrier, primarily ferrying tourists from Europe. While the respective cases can be seen within the framework of popular socialism in Tanzania and capitalism in Keyna, the result was intolerable economic stress. Kenya correctly saw itself earning sizeable profits for the Airways Corporation which were being frittered away by Tanzania's demand for uneconomical domestic air service.(9)

With the railways the problem was not nearly so visible, and was further clouded by being coupled with problems of the East African Harbours Corporation, as well. The two international ports of the Community were Dar Es Salaam, Tanzania, and Mombasa, Kenya. The former served Tanzania as well as Zambia, but was regularly overloaded, especially since the completion of the Tarzara Railway in 1974. Mombasa, on the other hand, served Kenya, Uganda via the Mombasa-Kampala Railway, as well as northern Tanzania via the Mombasa-Moshe rail line. Further, because of the alternative transportation available and the absence of great volumes such as Zambian copper, Mombasa was generally accessible. Coupled with the greater level of economic activity in Kenya, the lion's share of imports passed through Mombasa. This geographic-infrastructural benefit was not initially of Kenyan design and could not easily be modified. Uganda was geographically prevented from sharing this business, and Tanzania has been seeking to improve the port facilities at Dar Es Salaam for some time.

The underlying railway problem, however, which reached deeper into the political and economic life of Kenya than any previously cited, lay with highway competition. Traditionally the railway had charged relatively low rates for transport of raw materials and relatively higher rates for manufactured goods, consistent with the objectives of mercantile exploitation as practiced by the British. This gave the railway a disadvantage compared to highway transport as Kenya's importation of capital goods and consumer products increased as a result of continued capital investment and rising affluence. Furthermore, the ownership of the highway transport service, KENATCO, according to repeated unconfirmed reports was in the hands of influential politicians who exerted their considerable influence to effect preferential regulations and treatment for highway versus rail transport. Consequently, while rail capacity regularly lay idle, foreign exchange was consumed importing highway transport equipment from Britain (perhaps even at uncompetitive prices) which was then put into service at higher cost than existing rail facilities, thus raising commodity costs and lowering productivity. In addition, in this age of energy shortage and consciousness, highway transport imposed an added burden upon Kenya's foreign exchange balance by requiring additional petroleum imports. The political nature of this decision, while inherently consistent with other aspects of the Kenyan political-economic structure, is also symptomatic of the problems one uncovers in applying cost-benefit (supposedly rational) analysis to decisions in an elite system. Since it is the objective of the political-economic elite to maximize their relative advantages--which is already considerable--the vast majority of the population bears the cost.

Often in the post-Cold War age, when Africans confront a problem, an external conspiracy is suspected. Does a sinister web of intelligence agencies, multinational conglomerates, and capitalist exploitation take shape upon examining the external relations of the Community? The prime suspect, of course, would be a cabal of developed countries seeking to preserve cheap raw material sources, maximize markets and investment opportunities for manufactured goods, and preserve the relationships established during the previous colonial empires. This author begins with a skepticism toward all conspiracy theories, and finds no reason to alter that in examining the Community. Consistent evidence to sustain that charge is lacking. This is not to deny that, for example, British, America, and Japanese investors in East Africa all operated with a similar mindset--that of making profits with no particular commitment to disbursing wealth throughout the society. The resulting socio-politico-economic attitudes and practices are destructive of most of the objectives of a system bent upon genuinely improving the lot of its population and in developing participatory institutions. Nonetheless, whatever one may feel about the profit motive as a development incentive, intellectually one cannot sustain a conspiracy indictment in terms of the EAC simply on the basis that all the culprits were after a profit.

Nor is this to suggest that developed countries have exercised uncommon restraint in their dealings in East Africa. For example, as indicated above, recent transactions between the British and East African--now Kenyan--Railways suggest that factors other than usual business considerations entered into the awarding of the contracts.(10) It is generally believed in Kenya, at least, that the African managers and directors of international businesses are no more than fronts--even if well-rewarded--for the international operations which provide the capital and reap the long-term profits.

There is yet another political aspect to the demise of the Community. As one West African diplomat termed it, in the "first flush of independence" it is very difficult for newly sovereign states to participate in joint decision-making, especially when the express implications of that cooperation are the increased surrender of unilateral decision-making to a supra-national institution. The exercise of the long-sought political independence is too precious to be risked on the uncertain benefits of joint approaches to political or economic problems. This is especially true when ideological as well as economic objectives are still being formulated. Consequently, very often form is more important than substance: It is more important that the ambassador of a new country be accorded his full privileges than that the country be expected to develop a detailed position paper on an international issue. So when the three East African states merged their efforts in even so limited a way as through the Community, there was the expectation that shared decision-making was politically premature. In this connection it is interesting to note that the most advanced version of shared decision-making is the European Community, an example of regional integration which includes some of the oldest surviving states on the face of the earth.

This observation suggests a theoretical digression which may be useful in formulating expectations regarding integration activity in developing areas. Given the undeniability of the importance of exercising sovereignty in the "first flush of independence" it appears most likely that there is a process of aging--maturing perhaps--before states are politically willing to surrender a significant degree of sovereignty in favor a joint decision-making. This suggests the theoretical avenue that there is a casual connection between the age of states _qua_ states and their propensity to engage in meaningful joint supra-national decision-making.(11)   Thus, to expect much in the way of integration activity in developing areas is ill-advised, simply from a theoretic viewpoint.

Then there is the economic aspect of the Community's problems.   Suffusing any analysis of the Community is the overriding reality of Kenyan supremacy. While it is of course impossible to say what would have been had events evolved differently, it is indisputable that the economic data for Kenya is, and has been, uniformly positive, especially in contrast to Tanzania or Uganda. Building upon a distorted base for interstate trade stemming from the colonial period--90% of that trade was Kenyan trade with the other two states, by 1974 Kenya accounted for 48% of all East African external trade.(12) At the same time Kenya was responsible in that same year for 73% of East Africa's foreign trade deficit. Over 48% of all imports during the first three-quarters of 1975 went into Kenya, with 44% going to Tanzania and the remaining 7.4% going to virtually bankrupt Uganda.   Comparing the two major importers, Kenya led in every category of imports except food, indicating Tanzania's non-self-sufficiency in this vital developmental objective.(13) Kenya continued to enjoy a lion's share of Community wealth. Some additional examples will illustrate: Though the three states have roughly equal populations (Kenya 14 million; Tanzania 16 million; Uganda 12 million), in 1974 Kenya's trade was Sh. 10.4 billion out of a Community total of Sh. 21.9 billion; in January, 1973, Kenya received Sh. 104 million of income tax allocation (67.14%) out of a Community total of Sh. 154.9 million; September, 1975, sales of electricity (kwh)--a prime indicator of economic health--were Kenya 89.5 million; Tanzania 42.7, and Uganda 56.4.(14)

It is quite clear from the preceding analysis that while Kenya has enjoyed an unfavorable balance of payments in recent years, this has not been a deterrent to development. She is clearly able to raise the necessary credits to maintain this standard of activity resulting in her total public debt rising slowly from Sh. 1,709 million in 1968 to Sh. 2,115 million in 1972--a rise of Sh. 405.5 million (23.7%). This is compared to Tanzania's rise of Sh. 767.5 million (over 108%) (less than one-third attributable to China's investment in the Tanzam Railway), and Uganda's increase of 65%.(15)   Apparently Kenya has been able to manage and maintain a fairly well balanced economy for a developing state. Thus, the debt was growing at about 6% per annum (at unadjusted monetary rates), with the gross national product per capita growing at an adjusted rate of 4.1% per annum per capita.(16)

A prime rationale for any cooperative international economic effort is to achieve economy of scale. While there were undeniable benefits achieved in such Community activities as the corporations and income tax collection, in the private sector what benefits there were occurred through the expansion of Kenyan industry making available consumer products essentially to a small elite in Tanzania and Uganda.(17)   Consequently, the development of widespread popular support for Community activities based upon visible benefits did not develop--if it ever could have in such underdeveloped economies and societies. Given, for example, the literacy rates of 27 per cent for Keyna, 17 per cent for Tanzania, and 30 per cent for Uganda, it is not difficult to imagine that there would be a problem communicating effectively the benefits of the Community when they are perforce subtle if not complex.(18)

The law of comparative advantage was also substantially repealed for the Community by the imposition of an internal tariff, euphemistically termed a "transfer tax." The net effect was that Tanzania imposed a tax on imports from Kenya in accordance with the provision in the Treaty providing that if it had a fairly sizeable manufacturing capacity for that particular product it could levy a tax on imports from the other two partner states.(19)   As Helleiner points out, this device, while designed to equalize economic development among the three economies, achieved this by the device of diverting, not creating trade.   Tanzania collected Sh. 221 million in transfer taxes during 1970-74, 97.68% of which derived from goods being imported from Kenya.   Uganda being the middle state on the development spectrum could only apply the tax to imports from Kenya, and during a similar period it amounted to Sh. 231,547 million, an average of over Sh. 46 million per annum, very close to the amount collected by Tanzania. This did not deter Kenya's growth.

Each of the three states was hopelessly seeking autarky-to become self-sufficient in as many activities as possible rather than to become increasingly interdependent. The transfer tax was designed to further this objective, despite its being contradictory to the expressed objectives of the Community. For example, the plywood market in the Community in the early 1970's was such that the greatest economy could have been achieved with a single existing large manufacturing facility. What happened, however, was that more facilities were built in each member state, not for economic reasons, but for political considerations. This effectively negated the positive potential of the common market dimension of the Community in achieving economy of scale because the members were unwilling to bear the political cost.

Finally, there is the "failed triad" issue. In a three-member decision-making body the alternative to unanimity is one of three possible 2-1 splits which means that the second member of the majority can be seen by the minority member as siding with the "enemy," especially if there are persistent differences between two members of the triad. This has been true of the Community: Tanzania and Uganda have been at odds since Amin's violent overthrow of President Obote in 1971, and Kenya was seen by Uganda as siding with Tanzania too often. As a broader theoretical consideration, a "committee" of three is too small for long-term, far-reaching decision-making. The possible permutations of the majority are four: unanimity, Kenya and Tanzania, Kenya and Uganda, Tanzania and Uganda. Thus, the dynamics of political decision-making can become so constrained that problems are often maximized rather than ameliorated. The lesson: from a theoretical decision-making perspective, there should always be more than three participants in a regional activity.

* * *

Looking back over this array of problems, what can be seen most clearly of all is that there was no single clearly identifiable malaise which struck the Community. For the careful observer of this integrative effort, as well as any

74

other in developing areas, it should be clear that expectations must be conservative. Given the relative homogeneity, interplay of historical and environmental factors, and its good fortune, the European model establishes the outside parameter for integration efforts at this time. Certainly, no more can be expected in a developing area. Given the mixed experience of the East African exercise some minimum expectations can perhaps be posited as well.

It would appear that, at the least, while one cannot ascribe a single cause as being responsible for the demise of the Community, there are pre-eminent political and economic factors which must be incorporated in any post mortem: the dominance of the Kenyan economy and the internal political considerations which prevented decision-making in the interest of the Community at the expense of private entrepreneurs.

If one must ascertain a pre-eminent fatal flaw in the environment in which the Community operated, it would appear to be a combination of the gap--ideological, but also in terms of resources--between Kenya and Tanzania plus the extreme addiction to capitalism which operates within Kenya. The imprecision with which one can speculate on alternatives to the human course of events leads perhaps to this best conclusion: If all other factors had been operating positively, no one of the causes introduced here would have been sufficiently powerful to bring down the Community. But the combination of factors was too much for the fragile institution to accept. If a future enterprise is to be successful, it must at the outset be prepared to cope with these problems most of which will only disappear in the face of conscious political efforts in a spirit of greater cooperation than has heretofore been in evidence. Some will simply never go away and will have to be offset by the produced benefits of a Community.

* * *

There remains the question: What now? Recognizing all the caveats normally introduced in foretelling the future course of human events, especially in political Africa, it still is possible to venture some suggestions about the future course of events.

It is widely agreed, both publicly and privately, that the East African Community per se is dead. But there is also widespread agreement at least privately among both Community residents and foreign observers that the problems for which the Community was to have been a solution still exist and still demand solutions, and that a cooperative attempt at solution is desirable. Further, many observers, as well as theoreticians agree that a communal solution is the most cost-efficient approach. The problem is how to create an institution which can elicit or instill the political will which was lacking in the East African Community.

The first significant difference from the East African Community likely to emerge in a future integration effort is that it will be much more extensive.(20) Just as the United Nations' Economic Commission for Africa advocated at the outset of the Community, a new East Africa is likely to extend from Ethiopia to Mozambique encompassing up to a dozen members, depending upon transitory local political conditions at any given moment. There is an increasingly strong tie developing between Tanzania and Zambia, cemented by the railway. There also have been negotiations between Tanzania and Mozambique in recent months. Whatever is done in pursuit of a broadly-based wider community, however, must await a return to some level of order in Uganda and Ethiopia in particular. Some acceptable resolution of the expansionist objectives of Somalia must also be attained if the prospective community is to be East Africa in the broadest sense. Of course, the continuation of these problems cited above need not preclude a more limited community including the currently more stable southern portion of East Africa--perhaps Mozambique, Tanzania, Malawi, Zambia, Rwanda, Burundi, and Botswana could be the nucleus--if not the most logical economic entity.

Kenya, as the linchpin of the former Community, is likely to be central to any future arrangement because of both its geography as well as its level of economic development. However, as its present politico-economic isolation suggests, it will almost certainly have to move leftward (assuming that its neighbors, especially Tanzania, Uganda, Ethiopia, and Mozambique, do not make an unexpected and dramatic swing to the right. This, almost certainly, implies awaiting the passing of President Kenyatta's clique of business-political leaders who now decreasingly dominate the Kenyan political and economic scene under President Moi but who effectively dominated the economy of the Community prior to Kenyatta's passing. Before there can be the kind of negotiations which could lead to a new cooperative effort, however, the instability in the area of the horn of Africa--Ethiopian disintegration, Djibouti's precarious independence, and Somalian quarrels with its neighbors will have to be surmounted. It would be unfortunate if any successor organization were conceived, as it surely could be, as a pawn in a relatively transitory conflict as tilting the balance in one aspect of the conflict originating in the horn. Also, it goes without elaboration that Idi Amin's successor will have to be firmly in place before Uganda can participate meaningfully in any cooperative effort.

There are intangible conditions which must also exist, and they were well stated by Kenya's Foreign Minister, Dr. Manyua Waiyaki: "Political will, good faith..., political courage, respect for international laws, and a realistic approach to common problems in our region are the minimum conditions under which there can be political cooperation and understanding."(21) The chicken-egg question of integration is always: Does economic cooperation breed the requisite political will to make the community work--or must a favorable political climate exist in order for economic cooperation to flourish? Thus far the East African Community has not provided much insight to this dilemma.

Chapter IV

Footnotes

1. The author was in Nairobi for several months in mid-1977. Thanks go to Professors Domenico Mazzeo and Vincent Khapoya, then of the University of Nairobi, for their comments which have enriched this chapter. The writer, of course, assumes responsibility for its contents.

2. East African Airways Corporation, East African Railways Corporation, East African Harbours Corporation, and East African Posts and Telecommunications Corporation.

3. East African Agriculture and Forestry Research Organization, East African Audit Department, Directorate of East African Civil Aviation, East African Customs and Excise Department, East African Freshwater Fisheries Research Organization, East African Income Tax Department, East African Industrial Council, East African Industrial Research Organization, East African Institute of Malaria and Vector-Borne Diseases, East African Institute for Medical Research, East African Leprosy Research Center, East African Literature Bureau, East African Marine Fisheries Research Organization, East African Meteorological Department, East African Tropical Pesticides Research Institute, East African Trypanosomaiasis Research Organization, East African Tuberculosis Investigation Centre, East African Veterinary Research Organization, and East African Virus Research Institute. The Inter University Committee for East Africa is a special case.

4. See, for example, Julius K. Nyerere, Freedom and Development. Uhuru na Maendeleo. Nairobi: Oxford University Press, 1973.

5. See Allen L. Springer, "Community Chronology" elsewhere in this volume.

6. To indicate the extent of that gap two sets of data suffice. During the period 1964-1970, the percentage of Kenya's gross domestic product attributable to manufacturing ranged from 10.2 to 12.5%, rising rather

steadily.   For Uganda and Tanzania the figures ranged
between 5 and 7.9 with Uganda showing no increase.   The
World Bank reported in 1974 a GNP per capita of $170 for
Kenya, while Tanzania had $120 and Uganda $150.   GNP
growth rates per capita 1965-1972 were reported as   4.1%
for Kenya,   2.0% for Uganda, and 2.9% for Tanzania.
(Data from H. E. Grundemann, "Industrial Development in
East Africa: An Appraisal Including Possibilities for
Future Acceleration," a paper presented to the 1971
Universities Social Science Council Conference, Makerere
University, Kampala, Uganda, and "World Bank Atlas,"
Washington, D.C.:   International Bank for Reconstruction
and Development, 1974.) See also Mazzeo, Hazlewood, and
Ravenhill articles in this volume.

7. The other surviving institution is the East African
    Management Training Institute in Arusha, Tanzania, the
    headquarters location of the Community. This survives
    because it enjoys an externally-generated budget, and
    was consequently not effected by Community decisions,
    even the ultimate one.

8. Each partner subscribed 30.8% of its initial capital;
    the remainder was contributed by various external
    sources.

9. Differences of approach and need were reflected in the
    number of airfields served in the respective countries:
    Uganda had regular East African Airways service at one
    location, Entebbe, Kenya at four, while Tanzania pro-
    vided domestic air service to 20 locations.

10. My thanks to Professor Domenico Mazzeo for pointing
    this out.

11. This is explored in, inter alia, Joseph S. Nye, Peace
    in Parts (Boston: Little, Brown, and Company, 1971),
    as well as elsewhere in this volume.

12. In this connection it is, however, interesting to note
    that, according to 1974 data, of the ten leading trading
    partners with East Africa, Kenya led in trade with only
    four while Tanzania led with six. (Trading partners and
    their rankings in terms of trade with East Africa were:

with Tanzania: 1 United Kingdom, 2 United States, 4 Zambia, 7 Belgium, 9 Hong Kong, and 10 India, and with Kenya: 3 West Germany, 5 Japan, 6 Netherlands, and 8 Italy.)

13. Data from Economic and Statistical Review, No. 58, March 1976, Nairobi: East African Statistical Department. There is always a problem in valuing Kenyan foreign trade because of the flow of Ugandan goods through Kenya. This has been complicated in recent years because of a burgeoning black market in exporting primarily coffee from Uganda and the illegal importation of consumer goods.

14. Ibid.

15. Ibid.

16. Ibid and World Bank "Atlas."

17. See Arthur Hazelwood, Economic Integration: The East African Experience (New York: St. Martin's Press, 1975), especially Chapter 6, for a discussion of the negotiations, expectations, and failures in this arena of cooperation.

18. Data from The World Factbook 1974, Acton, Mass.: Publishing Sciences Group, Inc., 1974.

19. In addition to Article 20 of the Treaty for East African Cooperation, it is discussed in G. K. Helleiner, "Transfer Taxes, Tariffs and the East African Common Market," Dar Es Salaam: University College, Economic Research Bureau, No. 67.16, 1967.

20. Ethiopia, Zambia, Swaziland, Rwanda, Somalia and Burundi had explored membership in the Community at various times.

21. Interview in Africa, No. 73, September, 1977, p. 35.

CHAPTER V

Problems of Regional Cooperation in East Africa

Domenico Mazzeo

The collapse of the East African Community (EAC), put an end to one of the oldest, more sophisticated and relatively successful attempts at regional cooperation among developing countries. Initiated in 1917, by the early 1950's the process of cooperation in East Africa had evolved into a full-fledged "de facto" Common Market,(1) as well as a complex set of Common Services,(2) unparallelled in the history of regional cooperation among developing or industrialized cooperation among developing or industrialized countries. Economic interaction among the three East African countries was substantive at the time of independence. Intercountry trade amounted to almost one-quarter of total East African foreign trade.(3) The value added by the East African Corporations represented over half the value added by the transport sectors of partner states. Intercountry research budget was estimated at about two-thirds of the country-based research budgets in East Africa.(4) As may have been expected, after independence the importance of regional activities steadily declined in relation to nationally-based development activities. But the community, with almost 100,000 employees and assets valued at over 500 million Kenyan pounds was still in the mid-1970's an important economic force within the region.(5)

In addition to some significant achievements, other favourable conditions were expected to facilitate post-independence cooperation between the countries of East Africa, namely a common historical experience, cultural affinity, similarity of political institutions, and elite complementarity. In particular, the leaders of the three countries had repeatedly vowed to follow almost identical post-independence policies: African socialism, self-reliance, and non-alignment. They even envisaged establishing an East African federation. The heavier colonial presence in Kenya created these, a more acute land-hunger, a stronger administrative machinery, and a more diversified industrial basis. But the three countries were facing the same fundamental problems of nation-building and economic development. One may argue that the long experience of close association and the broad similarity of the countries would have generated a search for common solutions to common problems. Instead, the EAC, the only post-colonial major restructuring of cooperation in the region, did not survive to celebrate its tenth anniversary!

The end of sixty years of cooperation in East Africa may seem a disturbing phenomenon to those politicians and students of international relations who recognize the impor--tance of regional cooperation as an instrument of economic development, and greater independence from external forces. If regional cooperation is expected to provide greater opportunities for achieving economies of scale and a more rational use of the factors of production, nowhere could regional cooperation be considered more relevant than on the African continent. The majority of the countries have a relatively small market size and, consequently, a scarce potential for economic development, at least in the present world of highly competitive international economic relations.(6) Although the 1970's have not been favourable to regional cooperation and several regional schemes have been adversely affected by world-wide inflation and rising oil prices, regionalism remains a strong and stable trend in international relations. Stimulated mainly by technological development and its strategic and economic implications, the regrouping of countries is particularly evident in the industrial North. In a world of superpowers, aspiring superpowers and blocs, for the majority of the relatively weak states the only long-term alternative to regional cooperation may well be some degree of subjugation, irrespective of whether this will take military, political or economic form.

This paper investigates reasons for and consequences of the collapse of the EAC, with a view to drawing conclusions about the relevance of regional cooperation among developing countries. The analysis of the causes of the break-up of the EAC emphasizes intraregional institutional, economic and political factors, as well as extraregional influences. The consequences of this failure are discussed from both domestic and foreign policy perspectives of the ex-partner states. Such an investigation should be of interest to other third world regional groupings struggling for survival. It may also prove useful to East Africa, particularly after the recent change of government in Uganda, should negotiations take place for new forms of cooperation, eventually on a broader geographical basis.

(1) Factors responsible for the collapse of the EAC

The achievements of cooperation in East Africa may have

been remarkable and the break-up of the EAC regrettable, but the end hardly came as a surprise to any attentive observer of the East African scene. Since the mid-1950's, the history of East African cooperation was one of recurrent crises, motivated by a constant search for a more equitable distribution of benefits among partners. As in other parts of Africa, regional cooperation in East Africa had been conceived by the colonial power as an administrative and budgetary device aimed at reducing the personnel and financial cost of colonial rule, mainly in the interest of the settlers' community. This indirectly benefited Kenya, where the British administrative machinery was stronger and the settlers' community larger. As a result, Kenya was endowed with better infrastructural facilities and a more diversified industrial base. The appointment of territorial ministers in the mid-1950's, and the attainment of independence in the early 1960's, soon followed by the practical shelving of the idea of federation, was bound to heighten the concern for the protection of the interests of each of the three new autonomous actors. The question of distribution of benefits, almost irrelevant to the British government, became central to the survival of cooperation in the new political environment. From the late 1950's until 1977, cooperation in East Africa underwent three major reassessments, aimed at finding an acceptable solution to this question. The first two, in 1959-60 and 1964-67, yielded the East African Common Services Organization (EACSO) and the EAC respectively. In terms of policy formation and institutional arrangements these seemed, for a few years at least, an acceptable solution to the partner states. However, the third, in 1975-77, ended with the collapse of the EAC. EACSO, the last word of the colonial administration, emphasized financial compensation as an instrument of redistribution of benefits. But it soon became clear that independent Tanzania(7) and Uganda were more interested in balanced industrial development. The 1964-65 Kampala-Mbale Agreements,(8) were intended to address that need. Kenya's failure to ratify the Agreements precipitated a chain of unilateral decisions by Tanzania and Uganda, namely the imposition of restrictions on imports from Kenya and the establishment of national currencies, that could have promptly brought about the total collapse of East African cooperation. However, the benefits were still considered important, the echoes of the debate on federation were still in the air, and

the East African outlook of the Makerere-educated elite
was widely shared. None of the three governments was prepared to accept responsibility for non-cooperation. Over one
year of negotiations under the Commission for East African
Cooperation, during which objectives and institutions of
cooperation were reviewed, led to the Treaty establishing the EAC. In terms of new policies and institutions, the
Treaty was expected to provide a comprehensive answer to recurrent crises traditionally afflicting relations between
members, and to constitute a long-term solution to problems
of cooperation in East Africa. Did the community collapse
because the Treaty's provisions were inadequate to achieve
the aims of regional cooperation and satisfy the needs of
partner states? Or did new economic and political developments from within and without the region make the provisions
of the Treaty unworkable and the positions of partner states
irreconcilable?

a. Weaknesses of Community policies and institutions.

The Treaty provided the Common Services and the Common
Market with formal recognition and elaborate institutions. In
particular, the Treaty made the question of the distribution
of benefits, including balanced development, one of its
central concerns. Tanzania and Uganda had in fact been
claiming, particularly since the mid-1950s, that the more
diversified industrial basis and better infrastructural
facilities in Kenya, were to some extent due to the concentration there of the institutions and services for East
African cooperation. Debate on a more equitable distribution of benefits from East African cooperation intensified in
the mid-1960's. Shortly before the Treaty for East African
cooperation was being negotiated, economists attempted to
assess the costs and benefits of East African intercountry
trade,(9) regionally-based industries,(10) and Common Services.(11). This debate was not, however, conclusive.(12)
Indications were that Kenya generally benefited more than its
partners from the various regional activities, both in financial returns and employment opportunities, as may be seen in
Table 1. The equalization measures adopted before the Treaty
were mainly financial and were judged unsatisfactory by
Tanzania and Uganda. The 1967 Treaty put more emphasis on

Table 1: Estimated Distribution of Benefits from East African Cooperation among the Partner States of the EAC (Percentages)

		Kenya	Tanzania	Uganda
(a)	**Common Market**			
	Percentage share of intercountry trade (1)			
	1968	63%	11%	26%
	1974	77%	17%	6%
	Intercountry exports as % of intercountry imports (1)			
	1968	244%	30%	76%
	1974	373%	47%	12%
	Intercountry exports as % of exports to all destinations (2)			
	1967	33%	5%	16%
	1973	24%	7%	4%
	Percentage share of EADB approved loans, as at Feb. 27, 1973 (3)	22%	38%	40%
	Collection of Transfer Tax 1968-74 (4) (million of shillings)	Nil	54.5	38.7
(b)	**Common Services**[2]			
	Share of the contributions of the E.A. corporations to GDP, 1970	59.5%	26.8%	13.7%
	Estimated distribution of employment provided by the EAC, 1970-71	53.9%	31.7%	14.4%
	Estimated distribution of overall benefits derived by partner states from the GFS, 1969-70	50%	26%	24%
	Contributions by partner states to GFS expenditure, 1971-72	48.9%	28.6%	22.5%
	Location of GFS expenditure 1972-73	57%	29%	14%

1. Economic and Statistical Review, March 1975, p. XV.
2. Mazzeo, D. Foreign Assistance...., op.cit., pp. 32-33.
3. Ibid., p. 41.
4. Economic and Statistical Review, September-December, 1972, p. 121 (for 1968-69-1970-71); and March 1976, p. 136 (for 1971/72-1973/74).

new policies and structural adaptations.

A more equitable distribution of benefits from the Common Services was expected through the relocation of headquarters, a balanced purchasing and investment policy by the Corporations within each country, and administrative decentralization. The Central Secretariat was relocated in Arusha, Tanzania. Nairobi retained the headquarters of the Airways and Railways Corporations, while the headquarters of the Harbours moved to Dar es Salaam and the headquarters of the Posts and Telecommunications to Kampala, along with the East African Development Bank. However, the bulk of the activities of the Common Services and consequently of investment and employment continued in Kenya. This was the case of the General Fund Services, such as the major research institutes, the Directorate of Civil Aviation and the Customs, Income Tax, Statistical and Meteorological Departments. Particularly disturbing to the other partner states was the performance of the East African Airways. In early 1977, about 80% of its activities were estimated by Kenya to originate and terminate in Nairobi.

Coordination of policies in operating the Common Services, notably the Corporations, was seriously handicapped by the functional approach adopted by the Treaty. Not only were the various transport sectors enjoying too much autonomy, but within the same sector there was often more than one decision-making centre, e.g., in air transport, airport construction was a responsibility of national governments, while ground services were provided by the East African Directorate of Civil Aviation (a General Fund Service) and transport itself by East African Airways (an autonomous Corporation). The most acute conflicts between national and Community policies developed in land transportation: road transport remained a national responsibility, railway transport a Community responsibility. As a consequence, when a decision had to be taken whether to build or extend a road or a railway economic criteria did not always prevail. The harmonization of transport rates for goods carried by roads or railways was also difficult to achieve. The delay in adjusting railway rates seems to have considerably reduced the ability of the railways to compete with road transport. The situation was further exacerbated by different attitudes toward land transport in the partner states, with Tanzania apparently favouring the railways and Kenya, perhaps because of heavy involvement of private interests, boosting road transport.

Major difficulties were also created by the Treaty's lack of clarity regarding the final objective of decentralization and, more specifically, rules that should govern relations between Community and country headquarters of the various Corporations. Relocation of the headquarters of the Corporations and the strengthening of the country headquarters of each Corporation were necessary to satisfy the request for a more equitable distribution of benefits among the partners. But was decentralization to be seen as a purely administrative measure or as the first step toward nationalization of the Corporations? Partly because of this confusion, relations between Community and country headquarters continued strained: Community headquarters wished to retain major decision-making power, while country headquarters were claiming almost complete independence. Except perhaps for the Airways, the Corporations had reached a development stage that justified a purely national administration of the services. More clarity on intended objectives and rules of procedures may have facilitated a more orderly process of nationalization, without affecting so negatively other aspects of regional cooperation.

Particularly since 1974, when the balance of payments of member countries sharply deteriorated, such a lack of clarity on the objectives of decentralization, coupled with the above mentioned functional approach, gave birth to the most publicized difficulty between Community and country headquarters of the Corporations: the transfer of funds argument, which brought about the so-called "financial" crisis and the final break-up of the Corporations. It is well known that the East African Harbours Corporation and the East African Posts and Telecommunications Corporation have traditionally run at a profit. The East African Airways was one of the few airways in the world to make profits during the 1960's and, with the exception of a couple of years, even during the 1970's. The only Corporation traditionally in deficit was the Railways, mainly for the reasons explained above. Still at the end of April, 1975, among cries of imminent financial collapse of the Corporations, the figures for cash holdings at Community and country headquarters for each of the Corporations were in the black. This is still true, if one takes into account cash required to meet domestic and international obligations, except for the Railways, which needed roughly an additional fifteen million shillings. The Corporations jointly enjoyed a surplus, as shown in Table 2. If one prefers facts to words, it is therefore not difficult to conclude that even the crises of the Corporations were more political than financial.

To ensure a more equitable distribution of benefits from the Common Market, besides retaining industrial licensing, the Treaty envisaged three new measures: the adoption of a transfer tax(13), the harmonization of fiscal incentives, and the East African Development Bank (EADB)(14) measures aimed at stimulating a more balanced industrial growth and consequently reducing imbalances in intercountry trade in manufactured goods. The transfer tax was intended to give a temporary protection to infant industries in Tanzania and Uganda, while providing an additional source of revenue. The harmonization of fiscal incentives could have helped to minimize the danger of unfair competition in investment policies and eventually to direct investments toward the less industrialized members of the EAC. The East African Development ment Bank was expected to play an active role in balanced industrial growth of the region. Results, however, did not live up to expectations.

The impact of the transfer tax in redressing imbalances is far from clear. Tanzania was able to keep under control the volume of its deficit with Kenya and to reverse its position with Uganda. But whether these developments resulted from the imposition of the transfer tax or, for instance, from the policy of the Tanzania State Trading Corporation, is difficult to determine, the more so, knowing that the imposition of the transfer tax did not prevent the Uganda deficit in trade with Kenya from increasing steadily. In any case, the problem with the transfer tax was that it may have been successful only by partially defeating the aims of cooperation, that is by encouraging duplication instead of diversification of industries.(15) Of the other two measures, the harmonization of fiscal incentives never emerged from the vicious circle of investigations and reports. No final agreement had been reached on the subject at the time of the break-up of the Community. The East African Develop-

Table 2: Financial Position of the E.A. Corporations,
End of April, 1975[1]

(Million Shillings)

Cash Holdings:	EARC	EAHC	EAP&TC	EAAC	Total
Kenya Headquarters	+32.5	+175.8	+16.0	+-10.2[2]	+224.3
Tanzania Headquarters	+35.0	+53.3	+13.0	+35.0	+136.5
Uganda Headquarters	+7.0	-	+7.5	+45.0	+59.5
Community Headquarters	-10.0	+7.6	+2.2	-10.0	-10.2
Total	+64.4	+236.7	+38.9	+70.0	+410.1
OBLIGATIONS (Domestic and Foreign)					-360.0
BALANCE					+50.1

1. Table drawn by the author on the basis of information provided in The Weekly Review, May 19, 1975, pp. 15-16.

2. The Kenya headquarters of the EAAC was said to be in a deficit of Sh. 10 million, "because" of commitments by Community headquarters. We have preferred to assign the deficit to the Community headquarters.

ment Bank, on the other hand, became operational and allocated its resources as planned. But it had neither the financial nor the legal power to influence the growth of regional industries. Investments were an insignificant share of industrial investments within the region. Further, the Bank had no authority to refuse loans for projects, which may eventually have duplicated existing industries in other states.

Functioning of the Common Market may have also been handicapped by some major lacunae such as the little emphasis on cooperation in the field of agriculture and monetary policy. The author has always found puzzling the fact that the industrial countries of the European Economic Community made a common agricultural policy one of the cornerstones of their cooperation, while regional groups of developing countries pay so little attention to cooperation in the agricultural sector, which makes up a good share of their gross national product and provides employment to the majority of their population.(16) The lack of coordination of monetary policy since the break-up of the East African Currency Board in 1965, and particularly since 1972, hampered considerably the Common Market. Common currency is certainly not a prerequisite for the creation of a customs union or even a common market as the experience of other regional groupings indicate. Even free convertibility of currencies is probably not required, if alternative measures are taken, as in Comecon. But it is hard to see how meaningful cooperation could develop between countries with such fluctuating and unreliable exchange rates as occurred in East Africa during the 1970's. The legal fiction of parity between the Kenyan, Tanzanian and Ugandan shillings was retained, while the market value of the three currencies continued to diverge. As a result, it became even more imperative to have the balance of intercountry trade settled in hard foreign currencies, greatly reducing the advantages of the Customs Union. Financial transfers were in fact so severely curtailed as to jeopardize the flow of intercountry trade or even transfers of income by Community employees.

A development complicating the life of the Common Market was the creation of the State/National Trading Corporations. One could argue that the existence of State Trading Corporations was bound to have negative effects on intercountry trade, on the assumption that trade grows better when it is "free". However, as the experience of the East European countries proves, trade can grow even faster when it is planned. It is not therefore the existence of State Trading Corporations that hampered intercountry trade in East Africa, but the lack of coordination between partner states concerning the activities of these Corporations generally and their role in intercountry trade in particular. Another development that negatively affected intercountry cooperation was the widening gap in income tax policy between partner states, notably since the late 1960's, as well as the break-up of the East African Income Tax Department in 1973. This Department was a collector of taxes, not a policy-making body. Decisions on income tax policies rested with partner states. However, these policies that were almost identical before independence began to diverge afterward. It was this growing divergence that fundamentally affected intercountry cooperation, rather than the actual break-up of the Department. Nevertheless, this break-up had a negative psychological impact as a further sign of the strength of the disagregating forces at work within East Africa, while eliminating one of the autonomous sources of revenue of the General Fund Services.

One could argue that equalization measures may have succeeded and the Treaty's inadequacies may have been corrected in time, if the institutional machinery functioned properly. The Treaty was one of the most structured answers to regional cooperation ever given by any group of developing countries. The highest decision making body, the Authority, consisted of the three heads of state assisted by the three East African Ministers. A Central Secretariat was established under a Secretary General. Five ministerial councils were created, primarily with advisory and coordinating responsibility.(17) The most innovative element was the East African Ministers, who in their triple capacity of assistants to the Authority, heads of the three main branches of the Secretariat, and chairmen of the councils, were to be in the living link between regional concerns and national interests of partner states. The Treaty also envisaged a Common Market Tribunal, besides retaining the East African Legislative Assembly. But however diversified and impressive it may have looked, the institutional machinery of the EAC lacked autonomous decision-making power. One could hardly object to the fact that decisions were taken by unanimity or consensus, not so much because in a Community of three members majority decisions are probably inappropriate, but mainly because in peaceful interstate relations the best way to secure compliance is through consent. On the other hand, it may have been unfortunate that the EAC lacked a more truly "regional" body such as the Commission of the European Community or the Junta of the Andean Group. In particular, the composition of the Authority, the major decision-making organ, was probably inappropriate. A collective body, made up of the Presidents, could have certainly served a useful purpose as an appeal board, but as the major decision-making organ, it increased the danger of instability and of transforming personal rivalries into national conflicts. Disagreement between ministers can be overcome more easily by presidential intervention. Ministers can also more easily be removed. Further, to give presidents the final say may discourage too bold initiatives by ministers for fear of being disavowed by their Presidents. Events in East Africa suggest that fundamental responsibility for regional cooperation should eventually rest with ministers rather than with Presidents. However, taking into account the present configuration of political development in Africa, with emphasis on nationbuilding and the concentration of power in the head of state as symbol of the nation, its feasibility is doubtful. In any case, with the Authority not meeting since 1971, the whole machinery for cooperation, notably the councils and the secretariat, lacked direction and atrophied.

At the same time, the inadequacy of the Treaty's provisions and institutional weaknesses should not be overemphasized. The utility of an instrument depends, to a good extent, on the ability of its makers and users. In many respects, the scope of cooperation and the institutions of the EAC compared favourably with those of other regional schemes, including the European Community. For instance, if the EAC lacked a relatively autonomous decision-making body, it enjoyed remarkable financial autonomy.(18) The East African Legislative Assembly certainly had nothing to envy in the European Parliament. The fact that the EAC survived for seven years almost without any guidance from the Authority is an indication of the relevance of previous achievements of East African cooperation, the suitability of most of the components of the institutional machinery, and the commitment and ability of Community officials, notably those in high positions, like the Secretary-General and the East African Ministers.(19)   A major weakness of the decision-making process of the EAC is not to be found in the "politization" of its institutions, but in the "personalization" of power in the Authority.

Another general source of fundamental difficulties for the EAC was the uneasy compromise between two different approaches to cooperation: the more commercialist ("free trade") approach, sponsored by Kenya, and the more developmentalist ("planned") approach, supported by Uganda and particularly Tanzania.   This created a basic disagreement from the beginning as to interpretation of the Treaty and the final objectives of cooperation. The disagreement affected the functioning of the Common Services and the Common Market. Implications of the railroad competition have already been mentioned.   The Airways Corporation was also negatively affected by the opposing concerns of Kenya, giving priority to the more profitable international flights, and Tanzania, seeking to expand domestic flights. The disagreement was even more pronounced in relation to a policy of balanced industrial growth.   For Kenya, the measures adopted were a maximum concession. For Uganda and particularly for Tanzania, they were a first step, the final objective being a regional industrialization scheme implemented through an East African Industrial Development Corporation.   Because of different development approaches, it may have been very difficult to solve this issue. The deterioration of the political climate made it practically impossible not only to solve this issue, but even to review the functioning of the Community.(20)   In February 1975, Kenya formally called for a revision of the Treaty.   The report of the EAC Treaty Review Commission was submitted in November 1976, apparently without any positive recommendation.

The foregoing analysis clearly suggests that the EAC may have survived and expanded only if it had been more capable than its predecessors, the High Commission and the East African Common Services Organization, to serve better the national interests of partner states by achieving a more equitable distribution of benefits, notably regarding industrial development.   The fact that distribution of benefits became an issue could be considered in itself an indication of the existence of a development gap between partner states, that is an unequal capacity to take advantage of the opportunities opened up by regional arrangements. To bridge such a gap and consequently achieve a more equitable distribution of benefits from intercountry cooperation, greater harmonization of partner states' development policies was eventually needed. Unfortunately, despite basic similarities in conditions and stated objectives at the time of independence, by the mid-1960's the three countries began to follow increasingly divergent development paths. This added to the difficult problems arising from a development gap the even more untractable problems arising from the gap in development policies. Within these two gaps lie the root-causes of the collapse of the EAC.

b. Unfavourable economic and political developments
within the region.

It is widely acknowledged that regional cooperation between partners at different levels of economic development is more likely to end in failure, unless positive measures are taken to assist the less developed members. In the EAC, Kenya was the "more developed" and Tanzania the "least developed" member. Particularly in per capita income growth and industrial activities, Kenya has led East Africa since the mid-1950's. However, in other indices of distribution, Tanzania and Uganda have probably performed better than Kenya. In mainly agricultural countries, the share of small farms in monetary agriculture is a good indication of distribution of wealth within the country. In 1960 such a share was 20% in Kenya, 58% in Tanzania and 80% in Uganda. The respective figures in 1972 were 52% in Kenya, 74% in Tanzania and 77% in Uganda. Despite the increased share of small farms in monetary agriculture in Kenya, about half the marketed agricultural production in the country is still in a few hands! At the time of independence the income per capita of the African population was also higher in Tanzania and Uganda.(21) As shown in Table 3, there is little evidence that the gap between Kenya and Tanzania widened since the creation of the EAC. Growth rates in gross capital formation, government revenues and expenditure, and paid employment, for instance, have generally been higher for Tanzania during this period, although inflation rates were also higher

95

than in Kenya. In any case, Tanzania has been particularly successful in the 1970's in developing its manufacturing industries and increasing its share of intercountry exports. Kenya, on the other hand, expanded considerably its agricultural production, notably export crops, obtaining by far the best results in export trade outside the Community. In 1973, for the first time, Kenya took the lead over its partners in the volume of foreign exports. As indicated earlier, Kenya also continued to enjoy greater advantages from the Common Services. Table 3 shows that the sick member of the EAC was Uganda. Her economic position within East Africa began to deteriorate in the mid-1950's, and became critical after the military coup. By 1974, Uganda had ceased to be an economically active partner, as figures in Tables 1 and 3 clearly indicate. Uganda's share of intercountry trade, for instance, dropped from 26% in 1968 to 6% in 1974, while during the same period Tanzania's share went from 11% to 17%, and Kenya's share from 63% to 77%.

Probably more convincing is the evidence on the widening gap in development policies between the three East African countries during the life of the EAC. Scholars and the press have generally paid greater attention to differences between Kenya and Tanzania.(22) Events in Uganda were nevertheless of at least equal significance. While Kenya and Tanzania enjoyed political stability and continuity of leadership, their interpretation and continuity of leadership, their interpretation and implementation of African socialism, self-reliance and non-alignment diverged throughout the years. This is particularly evident in their respective land policies. In agricultural countries, land policy determines the structure of society. Aiming at a structural transformation of political and economic relationships, the Tanzanian leadership took two important steps: nationalization of the means of production, notably the land, as the major instrument of nation-building, economic development, and social justice; and separation of political and economic power. The policy of villagization, based on collective ownership of the land and accompanied by an adaptation of the educational system to the needs of a peasant society, represents a determined effort to bring agricultural and industrial development, physical infrastructures and social services to the countryside, where the majority of the population lives. The government of Kenya, instead, by the mid-1960's had abandoned

Table 3: Economic Performance of EAC Partner States, 1967-76

	Kenya	Tanzania	Uganda
(a) General Indicators, 1967-74[1] (Overall percentage increases)			
Gross Domestic Product	100%	100%	n.a.[2]
Gross Capital Formation	130%	140%	n.a.[2]
Government Revenues	260%	340%	-16%
Government Expenditure	280%	330%	3%
Paid Employment	34%	38%	24%
(b) Trade (1969-74)[1] (Overall percentage increases)			
External			
Exports	250%	50%	60%
Imports	300%	380%	0%
Interstate			
Exports	74%	110%	-150%
Imports	13%	31%	79%
(c) Production[3]			
Principal crops: Coffee, Cotton, Sisal and Tea ('000 metric tonnes)			
1967	135.8	338.4	n.a.[2]
1976	191.6	236.0	n.a.[2]
Industrial Output			
Cigarettes ('000 m. sticks)			
1967	2.07	2.04	n.a.[2]
1976	3.40	3.63	n.a.[2]
Beer (m. litres)			
1967	48.8	23.3	n.a.[2]
1976	165.6	69.5	n.a.[2]
Cement ('000 tonnes)			
1967	433.6	146.9	n.a.[2]
1976	971.1	244.0	n.a.[2]
(d) Cost of Living Indices[3]			
Middle			
1970	100	100	n.a.[2]
1976	191	221	n.a.[2]
Wage Earners			
1970	100	100	n.a.[2]
1976	210	294	n.a.[2]

1. Percentages calculated by the author from data contained in the E.A. Statistical Review, E.A.S.D., for the years under consideration.

2. Information not available in the sources referred to.

3. Annual Reports 1977, Bank of Tanzania & Central Bank of Kenya, Quarterly Bulletin of Statistics, Nairobi, March 1978. Tables from which these data were taken, have been kindly provided to the author by Dr. T.R.C. Curtin, Delegation of the European Communities in Nairobi.

any commitment to African socialism opting for an adaptation, if not a consolidation, of the "status quo" through a policy of Kenyanization, an open door to foreign investments, and formal education. Kenyanization of the economy, and of land in particular, meant a transfer from the settler community to the local elite, rather than a substantive redistribution of land.(23) By allowing public officials to retain their positions in the private sector, Kenya encouraged concentration of political and economic power in the same hands. Divergent policies are also evidenced in their respective educational, health and wage policies.(24) Results, however, did not necessarily meet expectations, and in practice differences were less pronounced than expected.(25) The two countries basically established mixed economies, with each claiming relative success in the general growth. Kenya could be particularly proud of its agricultural achievements and its ability to expand its exports outside East Africa. Tanzania succeeded in considerably diversifying its industrial basis and, during the life of the EAC, increased its share of intercountry exports of manufacturers, while the immediate result of villagization was a lowering of agriculture productivity(26), the sector to which Tanzania claimed to pay the greatest attention. Neither country succeeded in solving the more fundamental issues of bridging gaps between various provinces or between the city and the countryside, reducing unemployment, and upgrading real wages. During the last years of the EAC, differences between the two countries were more and more translated into ideological jargon. One is, therefore, tempted to conclude that differences were based more on expectations and perceptions than on realities, more on trends than concrete results.

Uganda has been characterized by instability and lack of leadership throughout its post-independence era. The absence of a popular leader or system of government brought a reliance on the army as primary instrument of power.(27) The result was the coming to power of Amin who for over eight years, adding cruelty to ignorance, subjected the interests of the nation and the state machinery to saving his career and the interests of his Sudanese mercenaries. Under the military regime, the Ugandan economy steadily deteriorated: the production of cash crops decreased and manufacturing practically halted.(28) The elite was systematically exterminated and administration broke down creating unprecendented

problems for the EAC and introducing new stress and conflicts. The coup of 1971 almost completely cut off Uganda
from playing a meaningful role in intercountry cooperation.
The headquarters of the East African Posts and Telecommunications practically returned to Nairobi from Kampala. By
1974, Ugandan exports to its partners had almost ceased.
Regional projects, such as the Soroti-based Civil Aviation
Pilot Training Project, were delayed and hampered. Agreement on nomination of Community officials became difficult
to reach. Working of the Authority was paralysed. An atmosphere of military confrontation soon developed between
the partner states, notably Uganda and Tanzania, culminating
in the border clashes of 1972 and renewed hostilities in late
1978, which ended in April, 1979, with the overthrow of the
military regime in Uganda. Further, the Ugandan coup stimulated the transformation of the region into a battle-ground
for influence by outside powers. Some Arab countries, notably
Libya and Saudi Arabia, cherished the prospect of weakening
Israel's position in Africa and adding perhaps a new country
to the Muslim family. Thus millions of dollars were poured
into Uganda each year to buy arms and pay mercenaries who
massacred the Ugandan population. The Soviet Union, eager to
penetrate deeper into Africa, was not ashamed to supply arms
and advisers.

Worsening relations between the three East African countries were matched by a growing spirit of recrimination among
the public. During the 1960's, favourable public opinion had
probably been as important as government initiative in keeping cooperation alive. By the mid-1970's, the behaviour of
the press in Kenya and Tanzania much resembled the Soviet or
Chinese Press. Which factors overrode in such a short period
the spirit of "Eastafricanness" within the region? First,
was the breaking up of the East African University in 1970.
The importance of Makerere in the formation of an elite with
an East African outlook is widely recognized. While the
decision to establish national universities could hardly be
criticized, the agreement to continue cooperation through the
exchange of teachers and students was not respected. Clearly, governments chose to use universities as a major instrument in nation-building, was rather perceived as opposition
to other nations. The negative consequences of the break-up
of the East African University were aggravated by the uncrit-
ical behaviour of the national media, more often ready to

emphasize differences than similarities between the countries. The young generations of academics and government
employees not only grew without an "East African outlook",
but almost with a feeling of despise and enemity towards
their colleagues in partner states. The lack of national
self-criticism in the press was particularly evident with
respect to the issue "who should be blamed" for the difficulties and final collapse of the EAC.(29) Based perhaps
partly on the inherent difficulties of cooperation, partly on
false images, and partly on determined plans of interested
sections of the elite in the three countries,(30) accusations and counteraccusations became increasingly persistent
and vehement. This may have convinced even the well-inten-
tioned politicans, committed Community officials, and sections of the public that divorce or at least separation was
inevitable.

c.   Extraregional influences.

     Individual countries and regions are vulnerable to ex-
ternal events, notably in economics. Worldwide inflation and
the monetary crisis of the 1970's exacerbated the economic
problems of most countries. Strains between members of
regional groupings, including the European Community, became more severe. But while the more developed European
countries seem to have succeeded in using the crisis as a
stimulus for further cooperation, the combined stress of
growing internal problems and an hostile international economic environment had an opposite effect upon the EAC, mainly
because of a higher degree of its members' external dependence. Inflated prices of imported machinery and oil were
mainly responsible for the worsening balance of external
trade of Kenya and Tanzania.(31) The sudden and unprece-
dented scarcity of hard currencies may have compelled these
two countries to curtail intercountry imports, consisting
primarily of consumer goods, and to refrain from transferring
funds to the corporations' headquarters.(32) The conduct of
foreign policy also became increasingly uncoordinated.
Diversification of external relations by newly-independent
countries is important, in order to lessen dependence on one
major power, and acquire greater freedom of diplomatic maneuvering and economic interaction. In a world of competing
powers and blocs, however, this entails the risk of opening

zones of influence. During the 1970s, each of the EAC members became entangled with one of the three major powers.
Tanzania was involved in a bilateral cooperation and trade
agreement with China which affected its economic relations
with the EAC partner states. The military regime in Uganda,
for its own survival, chose Arab money and Soviet arms,
though still preferring Western goods. Kenya remained attached to its Western connections. The result was that each
member strengthened external rather than intraregional ties.
The divergent political affiliations, at least until the fall
of the military regime in Uganda, were probably more clearcut than their external economic relations, partly because of
the time lag between new political orientations and economic
realizations. The external economic relations of the EAC
partners, in terms of aid, trade and foreign investment
flows, are summed up in Table 4.

Assuming that aid and foreign investments contribute to
development or at least to growth, Table 4 shows that aid and
foreign investment flows did not narrow the eventual economic
gap between the members of the EAC and consequently did not
facilitate solution of the question of a more equitable
distribution of benefits. For the period 1960-76, Kenya
generally received a greater amount of aid than either of its
two partners particularly from multilateral sources, except
from 1973 to 1976 inclusive, when, interestingly, Tanzania
got more bilateral assistance from Western countries. Was
this a sign of the growing confidence of the capitalist West
in socialist Tanzania or simply an indication of Western
perplexities as the change of leadership approached in Kenya?
Uganda received considerably less than its two partners,
though the drop in bilateral assistance was notable beginning
in 1973. The major Western donors for the three countries,
however, remained the United Kingdom, the United States and
the Federal Republic of Germany, in that order, at least
until the early 1970's. Contributions of the socialist
countries were relatively small, except in Tanzania, owing to
the 200 million dollars provided by China for the construction of the Tanzam Railway. Comparative data on foreign
investments are incomplete, but it is well known that multinational capital and personnel prefer the greater opportunities and comfort offered by Kenya. Trade flows, from 1969 to
1974, reveal that Kenya has been most successful in achieving
diversification in the destination of its foreign exports,

Table 4:   External Economic Links on the EAC Partner States

(a)   Official bilateral and multilateral financial assistance
        to the governments of Kenya, Tanzania and Uganda, 1960-76

        (Disbursements (net), million of U.S. dollars)

	Kenya	Tanzania	Uganda
1960-70 [1]			
Bilateral	650.5	656.0	283.8
DAC[2] countries	588.5	374.0	252.8
FRG	36.4	37.8	16.6
UK	413.5	179.4	175.7
USA	91.7	74.5	42.5
Others	46.9	82.3	18.0
Socialist Countries	62.0	282.2	31.0
Multilateral[3]	202.5	140.9	74.7
World Bank Group	172.4	114.0	56.2
IBRD	71.4	42.2	8.4
IDA	83.3	67.2	44.3
IFC	17.7	4.6	3.5
UNDP/SF	17.4	13.0	9.8
UNDP/TA	3.9	7.2	3.3
WHO	3.7	2.9	2.0
Other UN agencies	5.1	3.8	3.4
Afr. Dev. Bank	1.6	1.2	0.2
GRAND TOTAL	853.0	796.9	368.5
1971-76 [4]			
Bilateral (DAC countries)	561.0	791.0	71.2
1971	69.5	51.4	20.2
1972	62.8	53.8	21.6
1973	80.6	91.0	9.0
1974	104.5	141.0	6.7
1975	105.6	233.5	4.5
1976	138.0	220.3	9.2
Multilateral	409.8	266.7	65.3
1971	27.8	19.7	11.1
1972	45.4	23.5	7.7
1973	77.5	19.0	7.9
1974	54.7	30.4	10.3
1975	97.0	107.4	15.1
1976	107.4	66.7	13.2
GRAND TOTAL	970.8	1,057.7	136.5

1.   Source: Mazzeo, D. Foreign Assistance...op.cit., p. 191.

2.   Development Assistance Committee of the Organization for
     Economic Cooperation and Development, Paris.

3.   Data cover the period 1946-71; the bulk of multilateral con-
     tributions, however, were also provided mainly after the
     independence of the three countries.

4.   Source : OECD, Geographical distribution of financial flows
     to developing countries. Data on disbursements, 1963 to 1976
     OECD, Paris, 1978, pp. 120-21 (for Kenya), 226-227 (for

     Tanzania), 238-239 (for Uganda),

(b)   External trade of the EAC partner states 1969-74[5]
       (percentages)

(i) Direction of Exports	UK	USA	JAPAN	FRG	CHINA	OTHERS
1969						
Kenya	23.3	7.9	–	12.4	–	54.2
Tanzania	25.8	7.6	0.9	4.1	–	57.6
Uganda	22.6	23.7	11.7	3.2	–	38.8
1974						
Kenya	11.3	4.9	3.3	10.9	–	69.6
Tanzania	15.9	8.0	3.7	6.2	3.5	62.6
Uganda	18.2	24.2	9.6	5.4	–	42.6
(ii) Origin of Imports						
1969						
Kenya	31.2	7.5	8.0	8.2	1.0	44.1
Tanzania	26.6	5.8	9.2	7.9	5.6	44.9
Uganda	34.3	4.1	13.6	9.5	1.9	32.6
1974						
Kenya	18.1	5.9	11.5	10.3	1.2	53.0
Tanzania	11.2	7.2	9.2	8.8	11.6	52.0
Uganda	27.0	4.6	9.1	13.7	2.5	43.1

(c)   Private Capital Flows (net), 1969-76[6] (million of U.S. $)

	Kenya	Tanzania	Uganda
1969	4.3	13.8	16.8
1970	19.6	6.5	7.9
1971	11.5	8.6	6.9
1972	8.5	25.2	3.0
1973	41.8	18.0	-8.2
1974	19.8	-2.2	-9.7
1975	-10.2	-9.4	-6.6
1976	89.6	29.4	20.9
TOTAL	184.9	95.9	31.0

5.   Source: Economic and Statistical Review, for the years under consideration.

6.   OECD, Geographical Distribution, op.cit., ibidem.

These data are incomplete, mainly due to the unwillingness of some DAC members, notably Sweden and the U.S.A., to disclose the figures on private capital flows.
In August 1973 the author was promised by officials of the East African Statistical Department a report on foreign investments in East Africa. But it seems that this report has not come out yet.
In any case, assuming that the degree of incompleteness affects the three countries to the same extent, data show that Kenya is clearly favoured by private investors.

probably because of its more sophisticated manufacturing sector. More surprising, in 1974, Uganda and Tanzania were still more dependent than Kenya on British and United States markets for exports. Even in the case of imports, Uganda maintained stronger ties with the United Kingdom than Kenya and Tanzania. On the whole, however, the three countries' economic transactions with the United Kingdom have generally diminished, though traditional trade links with the West still prevailed in the mid-1970's. The major exception, again, was the sudden rise and decline of Chinese exports to Tanzania, in connection with the construction of the Tanzam Railway.

It is difficult to draw general conclusions on the possible role of external economic relations in the break-up of cooperation in East Africa. On the other hand, it is easier to cite examples of decisions, taken by member countries under the influence of external forces, which ran counter to the interests of cooperation. Such examples include the building of a tire factory in Kenya in 1965 that was expected to be allocated to Tanzania; construction of the Tanzam Railway(33) outside the authority of the East African Railway Corporation; and establishment in Nairobi of the International Laboratory for Research on Animal Diseases (ILRAD)(34) in competition with one of the most successful Community research institutes, the East African Veterinary Research Organization (EAVRO). Generally speaking, data on aid, trade and foreign investments suggest that even in the field of external relations economic factors may have exerted a less destructive impact on the EAC than political factors.

However desirable, the progress of decolonization in Southern Africa also indirectly contributed to loosen the links between the partner states. Tanzania's deeper association with liberation movements in Mozambique and Zimbabwe created new contacts and ideological affinities, perhaps encouraging Tanzania to take a tougher stand against Kenya even to the point of closing its border, and to look for new allies southward. This is not to suggest that Tanzania is attempting the creation of a new economic community with its southern neighbours. The negative experience of the EAC and the situation in the horn of Africa probably will make all Eastern and Southern African countries restrained in launching any new experiment in regional cooperation, at least for the next few years. It seems clear, nevertheless, that Tanzania has decided to strengthen cooperation with its Southern neighbours. In that respect, the Unity Bridge linking Tanzania and Mozambique is more than a symbol.

2. Consequences of the collapse of the EAC

Tension between former partners heightened as a result of the Community's demise. From October 1978 to April 1979, a full-scale war raged between Tanzania and Uganda, though one could argue that this war had at least the happy effect of putting an end to the Uganda military regime. Kenya resented as a highly hostile act, the closure of the border by Tanzania. Air space between the two countries has been recently reopened, but the land border remains closed halting almost all economic intercourse, notably in trade and tourism, between Kenya and Tanzania, and consequently between Kenya and Zambia. As can be seen in Table 5, this had disastrous effects on Kenya's exports of manufactures, which were heavily dependent on Tanzanian and Zambian markets. The stagnation of earnings from tourism in Kenya also to a good extent results from the border closure. In 1977, there was at least a 20% decrease in the number of tourists coming to Kenya. Hotels at the beach continued to do well, but those in the Nairobi area suffered. This suggests that Northern Tanzania was the strongest attraction for those Nairobi-based tourists interested in wild life, and that the border closure discouraged many of them from coming to Kenya. Reduced earnings from exports of manufactures and tourism, coupled with the decreased price of coffee and the outflow of capital which accompanied the death of Kenyatta are mainly responsible for the difficult financial situation in Kenya since mid-1978. The border closing was probably seen by Tanzania as bargaining potential during negotiations for the distribution of the East African assets and liabilities, since most of the physical infrastructures of the major Common Services were in Kenya. Negotiations among the former partners on the allocation of EAC assets and liabilities began almost immediately after the break-up. The experts' report on the subject is expected in 1979. Unless this question finds an acceptable solution, the changes of promptly normalising relations between the former partner states of the EAC, notably between Tanzania and Keyna, are minimal.

TABLE 5

Kenya's Exports Performance in Manufactured
Goods, 1976-77

		1976	1977
Industrial Supplies	K£	78.4m	64.7m
Machinery and Capital Equipment	K£	6.5m	1.2m
Transport Equipment	K£	4.0m	1.0m
Consumer Goods	K£	16.7m	14.6m
Total exports	K£	335.3m	480.2m
of which Food and Beverages	K£	159.5m	315.1m

Sources: Nation Economic Report, 1978/79, Nairobi, p. 17.

If the disruption of the Common Market affected Kenya more negatively, the financial and technical implications of the break-up of the Common Services, notably the Corporations and research institutes, will be more heavily felt in Tanzania and Uganda. After the collapse, Nyerere was quick to remind his people that more sacrifices were needed to restructure at the national level those services previously provided by the EAC.(35) More foreign loans and experts may be needed for a few years to come, prolonging this aspect of external dependence. Increased government expenditure for transport and communications may also contribute to further worsening of the balance of payments of the former partners. To run the services previously administered by the EAC new laws and new bodies were required in each country. The 1978

Kenya budget speech, for instance, mainly consisted of a sequence of proposals to put under national control those services once governed by the Community.

The most dangerous consequence of the collapse of the EAC may soon prove to be the development of an arms race. Owing to greater support for liberation movements in Southern Africa, Tanzania generally had a higher defense budget. Since the coup of 1971, the Ugandan regime felt threatened at home and allegedly abroad, and military expenditures went up sharply. The 1978/79 Kenya budget already indicates that defense expenditure is second only to education. If the Ogaden war was the immediate factor behind the Kenyan drive to strengthen its defense capability, the significance of the break-up of the EAC in this context should not be underestimated. The collapse of the Community, or more exactly the disappearance of the spirit of cooperation, was clearly responsible for Kenya's feeling of isolation.(36) Not only Kenya could no longer rely on the support of her former partners, she rather had reasons to consider them possible enemies.(37) Certainly, the Ogaden war taught Kenya a harsh lesson,(38) but the frantic Kenyan accusations against Somalia that were probably directed equally at other targets, namely at Amin's previous claims over Western Kenya. Any informed observers could hardly assume that Somalia would win against Ethiopia so heavily supported by Cuban troops and Soviet power. The expected military defeat of Somalia thus made her less and not more dangerous to Kenya. Besides, it was not the first time that Somalia and Ethiopia fought over the question of frontiers, but it was during the 1977-78 Ogaden conflict and after the break-up of the EAC that Kenya decided to considerably strengthen her military capabilities. One could proceed a step further and argue that the Ogaden war itself was partly a consequence of the failure of the EAC to survive and expand. The relatively golden age of good relations between Kenya and Somalia on the one hand, and between Ethiopia and Somalia on the other, coincided with the creation and the first promising years of the EAC, when both Somalia and Ethiopia expressed an interest in joining the EAC.

The break-up of the Community could also affect the domestic policies of its former members. The arms race, for instance, entails a reallocation of resources to a less productive purpose, directly affecting the well-being of the population at large, while the growing strength of the army increases the potential for military coups. In particular, one could argue that the break-up puts greater stress on national governments. The feeling of isolation could become more acute. Scarce resources may be less rationally used. One way of "exporting" problems or finding a "scapegoat" by blaming the other partner states or regional policies for domestic difficulties will be eliminated. Overall results could be greater internal instability in the former partner states of the EAC.(39) New difficulties and increased stress can also be used as instruments of nation-building, particularly through the manipulation of mass media by stimulating feelings of self-reliance and national unity. Exactly because the alternatives for "exporting problems" or "utilizing neighbours' resources" are diminishing, governments in the former partner states may have to face more squarely national problems, and become more responsive to the needs of their population and long-term interests of the country.

This seems to be happening with tourism. Tanzania is showing signs of a more aggressive and autonomous tourist policy, and seems more determined to improve her tourist circuits, mainly in the northwestern part of the country, one of the richest wild life regions on earth. Serious thought is now being given in Kenya to extend tourist facilities especially to the West and North, where tourist attractions are also considerable. Even more significant is the fresh look at the conservation of wild life resources evident in the December 13, 1977 announcement by the President that by March 12, 1978, not only the unauthorized killing but also the selling of wild animals trophies had to be terminated. This decision, motivated perhaps in part by the collapse of the EAC and the closure of the Tanzanian border, will hopefully prevent the extinction of many precious animal species in the country.

More generally, one may assume that the production pattern, notably the pace of industrialization will be affected. Unless new markets are quickly found, the rate of industrial development in Kenya may be slowed by the loss of the Tanzanian and Zambian markets in particular. On the other hand, greater protection of national manufactures may speed up industrial development in Tanzania,(40) not only in order to replace with local production goods previously imported from Kenya, but also to compete with Kenya for exports to other markets, notably in Rwanda, Burundi and Eastern Zaire.(41) This is made clear by the improvement of transport infrastructure between Tanzania and these countries. Of course, the competition between Kenya and Tanzania for markets for manufactured goods within the region could make relations between the two countries more tense for some time to come!

For the region as a whole, the effects of the collapse need not be entirely negative. New interest has been shown during the past couple of years in the revival of the 1965 Lusaka proposal to establish an Eastern African Common Market.(42) Talks have been resumed on the subject at the inter-governmental level, and possibilities of cooperation are more actively explored. In 1978, at a meeting in Lusaka, about fourteen Eastern African countries expressed their intention to establish an Eastern African Free Trade Arrangement. Several other inter-governmental meetings have already been held on this project, and negotiations are continuing. But the realities of the conflict in the horn of Africa, and the different development approaches of Kenya and Tanzania, suggest it may take time before even such a limited arrangement gets off the ground.

One may finally wonder whether the collapse of the EAC did not give Tanzania a freer hand to dispose of the military regime in Uganda and whether this could not contribute to the revival of a truly decolonized, purely indigenous regional cooperation effort. The idea of a revival of the EAC has been voiced, particularly towards the end of July, 1979, by both the Ugandan and Tanzanian Presidents.(43) At first, one may have expected the removal of the military regime in Uganda would facilitate the revival of the EAC. But the implications of the change of regime in Uganda are not clear yet. Years may be required to overcome the political and economic chaos in Uganda.(44) One should not forget that Uganda traditionally played an ambiguous role in intercountry cooperation. In 1963-64, for instance, Uganda was the staunchest opponent of an East African Federation. The impact of the circumstances of the change of regime in Uganda on the Kenyan-Tanzanian relations are also still uncertain. After the change of leadership in Kenya, notably since January, 1979, the President of Tanzania has made several overtures to Kenya, including the invitation at the end of May, 1979, to the Kenyan President to meet in Arusha, Tanzania, and the agreement to to the decision to reopen the air space between the two countries. As recently as the end of July, 1979, Nyerere reassured Kenya that Tanzania had neither the intention nor the capability to replace the important role that Kenya has traditionally played for the Ugandan economy. On the other hand, the open displeasure showed by Kenya against the Tanzanian "intervention" in Uganda and the support given by Kenya to the military regime in Uganda until the fall of Kampala did not increase the confidence between Kenya and Tanzania. There remains the fundamental fact of the two countries' divergent development approaches and the consequent competitive effort to influence the direction of development policies in Uganda. The cost of the recent war and the return of a victorious army could destabilize the economic and political system in Tanzania itself! In any case, the chances of reviving the EAC could be enhanced should the Eastern African Free Trade Arrangement fail to materialize or should Tanzania fail in its alleged determination to create a Community under its control comprising Mozambique, Zambia, Uganda, and eventually Burundi, Rwanda and Zimbabwe. Judging from African experience, one could say that if, after the elections, the government of Kenya realizes more fully the ominous implications of "isolation" and the situation in Uganda stabilizes, it will not be difficult for the three Presidents to agree to launch a new regional venture. But the success or failure of such a venture would certainly depend on whether the partners have learned some lessons from the collapse of the EAC.

Conclusion

The collapse of the EAC was clearly due not to a single factor nor to a single set of factors. Still, if the analysis of the East African experience has to be of greater value to other regional groups, one should assess the relative impact of these various factors. Did the Community fail because of Treaty weaknesses and personality conflicts? Or shall we look for explanation at more structural elements, such as the level and type of political, economic and societal development with the region? East African cooperation may have suffered from several Treaty handicaps, such as the lukewarm attitude toward coordination of development plans and industrial policies; the little attention paid to agricultural cooperation, and in particular the inadequacy of the measures aimed at a more equitable distribution of benefits.

A Treaty is, however, a compromise expressing a certain level of commitment by signatories at a given time. Treaties can be interpreted or amended according to the will of members and, eventually, to the vitality of the institutions set up to implement Treaty provisions. In the author's view, Community institutions were adequate to deal with their responsibilities on two conditions: one, that the national administrations of member countries be run efficiently; and, two, that the East African Authority fulfill its functions. During the life of the EAC, administrative efficiency in Tanzania probably did not improve and the administrative machinery in Uganda completely broke down, while the East African Authority was paralysed by personality conflicts between the presidents. Personalization of the decision-making process appears to have been a major factor responsible for the break-up of cooperation in the region. Unless the era of the king-president comes to an end, the chances of successful regional cooperation among developing countries, notably in Africa, may be slim.

Personal rule, on the other hand, seems to have its foundation on structural conditions prevailing in most developing countries, namely the problems of nation-building, the low level of industrialization, and the lack of organizational pluralism. The stress and urgency of nation-building demand the creation of a strong central government facilitating the identification of governmental with presidential power. The low level of industrialization, by making it difficult for pluralistic interest groups to emerge, equally strengthens the tendency toward concentration and personalization of power, breeding instability. Further, the low level of industrialization makes the allocation of industries and a programme of industrial specialization among developing countries extremely difficult to implement. On economic and social ground, each country wants to start with the simplest and most essential industries. Duplication follows and conflicts increase. It seems also, as in the case of Tanzania, that for a developing country the need to redirect imports from intercountry to extraregional sources grows, as the pace of its industrial development accelerates and the demand for technologically advanced equipment increases. Structural conditions prevailing in developing countries thus seem to be the root-cause not only of the personalization of power, but also of the difficulties in achieving more equitable distribution of benefits and controlling the negative impact of external dependence. Since these conditions are "common" to most developing countries, the question of the relevance of regional cooperation among developing countries must be raised. In this respect, one should clearly distinguish the relevance of theory or explanation from the relevance of the process of regional cooperation or the reality to be explained.

The relevance of the theory of regional cooperation is reduced by an adherence to rigid concepts not always linked to reality, for instance the concepts of "integration" and "supranationality", or the functionalist and neofunctionalist concerns with "depoliticizing" regional cooperation and "de-emphasizing" the importance of national interest. Existing regional schemes generally do not aim at replacing national actors, but at better serving their interests. The simpler concept of negotiation may thus be a more appropriate analytical tool for understanding the process of regional cooperation. The needed political will may, in fact, be more easily generated through a process of negotiation, which ensures the protection of national interests. Of particularly little use in evaluating the relevance of regional cooperation among developing countries are, in the author's view, the static concepts of "economic complementarity or competitiveness" and "trade creation or trade diversion", since the purpose of cooperation among "dependent" countries is obviously to "divert" trade from external to domestic or regional sources through a process of "diversification" of their economies aimed at creating either complementarity or competitiveness.

The experience of East African cooperation, suggests also that regional arrangements among developing countries are not irrelevant as instruments of economic development and peaceful relations among neighbours. There is little doubt that Tanzania and Uganda benefited from the Common

Services, while Kenya was certainly not compelled by the Common Market to slow down the pace of her industrial development! But how to facilitate not only a more equitable distribution of benefits from cooperation, but also a more accurate perception of such a distribution? A flow of information on the functioning of the equalization measures may help. Even more important perhaps, looking at the role of Makerere University in the creation of an East African mentality, would be some form of cooperation in education, to stimulate the growth of an elite with a regional outlook, capable of understanding each other's objectives and problems.

Finally, to be properly appreciated, the process of regional cooperation should not be considered as opposed to, but as part of a wider development strategy, combining national planning with regional, continental, and intercontinental cooperation of a South-South or North-South type. The question of "alternatives" in this respect, thus, sounds a little fictitious. And, it goes without saying, regionalism has to be seen in historical perspectives. A few years or a few decades are not a sufficient time to judge historical processes. It took about four centuries for the modern type of nationalism to assert itself universally. It may take as long for regionalism. It is important to understand the historical trend and act accordingly. Today, the trend towards the regrouping of countries on a regional basis is particularly evident among the industrialized states. Developing countries are aware of this trend. But are they determined to learn the lessons of disunity from the Greek and Italian city-states, and avoid undergoing additional centuries of dependence?

Chapter V

Footnotes

1. The major elements of the Common Market were:

    a. the free movement of the factors of production (labour, capital and goods)

    b. The industrial licensing system, which was agreed upon in 1948 and came to an end in 1973. The major aim of the system was to stimulate industrial development and avoid duplication of industrial activities within the region in a certain number of selected industries by giving them access to the East African Market. It began with the cotton textile industry in 1948. A few other industries, such as tobacco, footwear, beer and cement were added through the years. In 1967, it covered cotton and woolen textiles, glass, steel drums, metal doors and windows, and enamel hollow-ware.

    c. A common currency, issued by the E. A. Currency Board, from 1920 to 1965.

2. <u>List of Common Services Operated by the EAC</u>

    Corporations:

    > E. A. Airways Corporation (EAAC)
    > E. A. Harbours Corporation (EAHC)
    > E. A. Posts and Telecommunications Corporation (EAP&TC)
    > E. A. Railways Corporation (EARC)

    General Fund Services:

    Economic and Social Services:

    > E. A. Academy
    > E. A. Common Market Tribunal
    > E. A. Common Service Commission
    > E. A. Customs and Excise Department
    > E. A. Development Bank

E. A. Directorate of Civil Aviation
E. A. Income Tax Department
E. A. Literature Bureau
E. A. Meteorological Department

Research Institutions:

E. A. Agriculture and Foresty Research Organization
(EAAFRO)
E. A. Freshwater Fisheries Research Organization
(EAFFRO)
E. A. Marine Fisheries Research Organization
(EAMFRO)
E. A. Industrial Research Organization (EAIRO)
E. A. Institute for Medical Research (EAIMR)
E. A. Leprosy Research Centre (EALRC)
E. A. Trypanosomiasis Research Organization
(EATRO)
E. A. Institute for Malaria and Vector-borne
Diseases (EAIMvbD)
E. A. Virus Research Institute (EAVRI)
E. A. Veterinary Research Organization (EAVRO)
Tropical Pesticides Research Institute (TPRI)

3.   An impressive figure, if one considers that the average
      inter-African trade of the African countries was about
      3% of their external trade, during the 1960s. On the
      other hand, if Kenya's intercountry trade reached 33%
      of her external trade, Tanzania's intercountry trade
      ranged only between 4% and 7% of her external trade.

4.   Mazzeo, D. Foreign assistance and the East African,
      op. cit., p. 94. Common Services. Weltfrorum Verlag,
      Munich, 1975, p. 94.

5.   The Weekly Review (Nairobi), February 15, 1975, pp.
      6-8.

6.   One-third of the countries of the world are in Africa,
      a continent with about half the population of China and
      a combined GDP probably less than that of Brazil.

7.   Resulting from the merger of Tanganyika with Zanzibar
      in 1964. For simplicity, we will consistently use the

term "Tanzania", even when referring to previous years.

8.   The agreements proposed that new industries and new branches of expanding industries be located preferably in Tanzania and Uganda, and allowed these two countries to impose temporary restrictions against imports of manufactured goods from Kenya.

9.   Ghai, D. P., "Territorial distribution of the benefits and costs of the East African Common Market", in Leys and Robson, Federation in East Africa: Opportunities and Problems, 1965, pp. 72-82.

      Hazlewood, A., The East African Common Market: importance and effects, Bulletin of Oxford University Institute of Economics and Statistics, Vol. 28, No. 1, February 1966, pp. 1-18.

10.   Newlyn, W. T., Gains and losses in the East African Common Market, Yorkshire Bulletin, Vol. 17, No. 2, November 1965, pp. 130-138.

      Hazlewood, A. The "shiftability" of industry and measurement of gains and losses in the East African Common Market, Bulletin of Oxford University Institute of Economics and Statistics, Vol. 28, No. 2, May 1966, pp. 63-72.

11.   Hazlewood, A., The territorial incidence of the East African Common Services, Ibidem, Vol. 27, No. 3, August 1965, pp. 161-176.

      Green, R. H., East African Economic Union--an approximate balance sheet. Makerere University College, East African Institute of Social Research, Conference Papers, Paper 93, January 1966.

      Roe, A. R., The impact of the East African Treaty on the distribution of EACSO benefits, The East African Economic Review, Vol. 3, (new series), No. 2, December 1967, pp. 39-52.

12.   A summary of this debate is provided in Mazzeo, D., Foreign Assistance..., op. cit., pp. 30-40.

13. The tax was a duty that a partner state with a deficit in intercountry trade in manufactured goods was allowed to impose on intercountry imports of such goods. The maximum level of the tax was fixed at 50% the value of the common external tariff on similar goods. The tax could be imposed only if the deficit country was able to manufacture similar goods within three months from the imposition of the tax and if production would either cover at least 15% of domestic consumption or amount to a minimum of ₤100,000 per annum. The tax had to be terminated whenever the deficit country reached 80% balance in its overall intercountry trade in manufactures. In any case, no single tax could last more than 8 years and all transfer taxes should have been abolished 15 years after the coming into operation of the treaty.

14. The initial capital of the Bank amounted to Shs. 120 million, Shs. 40 m. from each partner states. In 1970 the EADB sold to six foreign banks additional equity shares of Shs. 9 million. In 1972, it received loans amounting to Shs. 109 million from the World Bank and the Swedish International Development Authority. Total funds available early in 1973 were thus 238 million shillings. According to the rules of the EADB, on a five year plan Tanzania and Uganda would receive 38.75% each and Kenya 22.50% of the resources of the Bank, as it has been the case so far.

15. The negative impact of duplication of industries on regional cooperation is obvious, even if the duplicated industries are expected to supply only the domestic markets of the less industrialized members of a regional group. Duplication necessarily curtails intercountry trade and in the long-run it may also increase rivalries between members for markets outside the region.

16. The fact that agricultural production in neighbouring developing countries is little diversified should stimulate even further the concern for cooperation in this field, in order to reduce the costs of purely national diversification policies.

17. The three branches of the Secretariat were: Finance and Administration, Common Market and Economic Affairs, and Communications and Research. The five Councils were: Common Market Council, Communications Council, Finance Council, Economic Consultative and Planning Council, Research and Social Council.

18. This was certainly the case of the self-contained or autonomous Corporations. But even the General Fund Services were directly financed by EACSO and later the EAC through half of the resources of the Distributable Pool of Revenues (the other half being used for purposes of financial redistribution). Under EACSO, the Pool was automatically replenished each year by 6% of customs and excise duties, and 40% of the revenue from income tax on manufacturing and finance companies in the three countries. The 1967 Treaty cut these percentages by half.

19. This is confirmed by the important positions top Community officials were given in their respective countries. For instance, the last Secretary General became Finance Minister in Tanzania, while the former Minister for Common Market and Economic Affairs was appointed Minister for Economic Planning and Community Affairs in Kenya.

20. It may sound ironic that the EAC was born in 1967, the year of the Arusha Declaration and died in 1977, the year of a major review of the performance of the socialist approach in Tanzania, a review that in certain quarters in Kenya was interpreted as a return to capitalism. Whatever the merits of such an interpretation, the economy needs time to reflect new political orientations.

21. Hazlewood, A., Economic integration--the East African experience. Heinemann, London, 1975, p. 6.

22. A. W. Seidman, Comparative Development Strategies in East Africa, The East African Journal, Vol. 8, April 1970, pp. 13-18.

The Weekly Review (Nairobi) notaby the September 15,

1975 and December 20, 1976, issues; and

The Economist (London), "Back to Back: A Survey of Kenya and Tanzania", March 11, 1978.

23. Apart from the "one million acres" resettlement scheme (of which about 800,000 acres have already been alocated) very little was done in this field, particularly until 1970. On the question of land policy in Kenya, beside the government Development Plans and annual Economic Surveys, consult:
Wanjohi, N.A.G., "Socio-economic inequalities in Kenya: the case of the Rift Valley Province", M.A. Thesis, University of Nairobi, 1976, 459 p.

Wasserman, G., "Politics of Decolonization: Kenya Europeans and the Land Use, 1960-65", Cambridge, Cambridge University Press, 1976, 225 p.

24. A comparative analysis is provided in The Economist, "Back to Back", op. cit.

25. Siloba wa Kwendo, "There is little difference between Kenya and Tanzania", The Weekly Review, March 8, 1976, pp. 6-7.

26. Antoniotto, A., L'esperienza dell' ujamaa in Tanzania; Africa (Roma), XXXII, 2, June 1977, pp. 177-199.
Once the human and physical foundations of a policy of villagization have been laid down, the long-term effects could be rewarding. But, apart from the weather conditions, several other factors were responsible for the disappointing short-term effects, in particular: the inappropriate location of some villages; the absorption of resources by an expanding bureaucracy and the cost of building physical infrastructures and social services in the villages; and the insecurity created by the upheaval of century-old traditions.

27. Mujaju, A. B., "The Dynamics of Leadership in Contemporary Uganda", Atlanta, Georgia, USA, Summer 1976, 43 p.

28. The Weekly Review, June 28, 1976, p. 25; and December

26, 1977, pp. 25-27.
Uganda survived economically simply because it is a rich agricultural country, more than 90% of the population live from agriculture, and about 80% of all marketed agricultural production is still in the hands of small farmers.

29. <u>The Weekly Review</u>, February 15, 1975; and December 13 and 20, 1976.

30. The Hon. Dr. R. Ouko, Kenyan Minister for Economic Planning and Community Affairs, in a public lecture on "Prospects of intercountry cooperation in Eastern Africa", University of Nairobi, February 26, 1979, rightly remarked that those Kenyans who drank bottles of champagne to celebrate the death of the EAC probably did not realize the importance of the Community to their country.

31. By the mid-1970's, only Uganda was still enjoying a favourable balance of external trade, owing probably to the fact that the manufacturing sector was stagnating and, consequently, there was no need to purchase more capital goods.

    Kenya expected to rely on its surplus in intercountry trade to meet a substantive part (about 50% in the 1960's and still about 33% in the 1970's) of its huge deficit in foreign trade. But when, in the early 1970's, the Tanzanian balance of foreign trade also became negative, Tanzania found it more and more difficult to continue to spend hard currencies in Kenya.

32. According to Community regulations, almost the whole deficit in intercountry trade and the transfer of funds for the Corporations had to be met in hard currencies.

33. The Tanzam Railway, conceived mainly to free the Zambian trade from dependence on the Portuguese territories, because a reality through a combination of Chinese generosity and political expediency. The construction of the Tanzam Railway affected negatively not only intercountry transport, but also intercountry trade. <u>The Weekly Review</u>, February 15, 1975, p. 9; and Decem-

120

ber 13, 1976, pp. 4-5.

34. From 1971 to 1973, the EAC Secretariat strongly opposed the creation of ILRAD, sponsored by the Rockefeller Foundation and other donors, mainly because EAVRO was already engaged in the same type of research that ILRAD was expected to carry out.

35. The Weekly Review (Nairobi), May 2, 1977, pp. 6-7.

36. "Kenya's growing isolation", The Weekly Review, May 23, 1977, pp. 5-10.

37. In March, 1976, a territorial claim on Western Kenya was made by the Ugandan authorities: Eastern Uganda had in fact been given to Kenya by Britain in 1902, when Ugandan territory extended some 20 km. from Nairobi! The closure of the border by Tanzania, in February 1977, was and is still seen by Kenya as a hostile act.

38. The Kenyan authorities seemed particularly shocked by the ambiguous stand adopted, during the Ogaden war, by the traditionally friendly Western countries, thus overlooking a simple fact: at least for the next ten or fifteen years the West will remain heavily dependent on oil from the Middle East and cannot risk a confrontration with the oil products, if these choose to support Somalia against Kenya!

39. The argument of the possible destabilizing effect of the break-up of the EAC on ex-partner states' domestic systems was elaborated in an unpublished paper by Dr. M. Mugyenyi, Department of Government, University of Nairobi, Summer 1977. In effect, one may wonder whether the collapse of the EAC did not contribute to destabilizing the military regime in Uganda; or whether the present regime in Kenya would survive, should Kenya lose the Ugandan and, consequently, the Burundi, Ruanda and Eastern Zaire markets.

40. Several other factors may have stimulated industrial growth in Tanzania, among them the increased pragmatism of the political leaders, the renewed confidence of the Asian community, and the higher share of the budget

121

allocated to the industrial sector.

41. This point was brought to the attention of the author by Prof. G. Mutiso, Department of Government, University of Nairobi, February 1979. More recently, reference to this was made at a press conference in Nairobi by deposed Ugandan president Y. Lule, The Weekly Review, July 20, 1979, p. 20.

42. This idea was strongly supported by the Economic Commission for Africa (ECA) between 1965 and 1968, almost in opposition to the creation of the EAC.   But after the Treaty for East African Cooperation was signed, there was general agreement in ECA and Eastern Africa to consider the EAC as the nucleus from which an Eastern African Common Market could develop.   The collapse of the EAC provided new impetus to the original ECA proposal.

43. The Standard (Nairobi), July 27, and August 4, 1979, front pages.   But the closure of the Tanzanian border is considered by the President of Kenya as a serious obstacle to the resumption of negotiations for the revival of the EAC. As the August 1979 meeting of the Commonwealth in Lusaka has shown, animosity between Kenya and Tanzania is rather on the increase.   See: "Nyerere blames Kenya", The Standard, August 8, 1979, front page; "Moi hits at Dar over border", The Daily Nation (Nairobi), August 8, 1979, front page.

44. To repair the damages of eight years of misrule, there is a need for a united elite and a united people.   This does not seem to be the case in Uganda. Without the presence of the Tanzanian troops, an outburst of civil war could not be excluded, thus providing the forces of the former dictator with an opportunity to attempt a comeback!   The Standard, August 6 and 7, 1979, front page.

CHAPTER VI

Economic Instrumentalities of Statecraft
and the End of the EAC

Arthur D. Hazlewood

I   INTRODUCTION(1)

There were few instruments of economic policy in the integration arrangements of the colonial period in East Africa. A major feature, indeed, was the absence of an instrument of policy, the import tariff, from the arrangements for interterritorial trade. It is true that it was always recognized that the charges imposed by the common services were not neutral in their effect, and there was a long history of controversy over the railway tariff. But taxation was not explicitly used to influence the relationships of the three territories: the principle of derivation applied in the allocation of both customs and excise and income tax revenues. However, the absence of a policy is itself a policy, and it was dissatisfaction with the alleged discriminatory effects of non-discrimination which led to successive changes in the integration arrangements and the introduction of additional instruments of economic policy. It was the failure of the policy instruments successively introduced to satisfy the member states which may be seen as the fundamental reason for the failure of economic integration in East Africa.

II   THE INDEPENDENCE SETTLEMENT

The colonial arrangements of the past had to be remodeled with the approach of independence for the East African countries. Change was essential once integration became voluntary and not enforced by the colonial power, because it was firmly believed in Tanzania and Uganda that the arrangements worked overwhelmingly to the benefit of Kenya. The customs union, it was believed, worked to the benefit of Kenya as the most industrially developed country of the three, and as the headquarters of the various common services were established in Kenya, the employment and income creating benefits of the services were believed also to accrue mainly there. The extent to which these beliefs were justified is not entirely uncontroversial, but it was the strength of the beliefs that counted. In 1961 a new structure for the government of the common arrangements was introduced with the establishment of the East African Common Services Organization, and a new instrument of economic policy was devised to deal with the unequal effects of the operation of the common market and the other common arrangements. The new policy instrument was a fiscal redistribution.

The fiscal redistribution was devised through the creation of a Distributable Pool of revenue into which a given
percentage of customs and excise and company income tax
revenues was paid. Half the receipts of the Pool was used to
finance the common services, and the other half was distributed equally between the three countries. The redistribution
was achieved, therefore, in two ways. The countries contributed to the Pool in proportion to their tax yields, but drew
from it in equal amounts, so that there was a redistribution
from the country with the highest tax yield. The countries
paid for the common services not equally, but in proportion
to their tax yield, though the redistributive effect of this
measure depended also on the distribution of the benefits
from the services.

The constraints imposed by the common arrangements
became irksome as the newly-independent governments began to
pursue more active, nationally-oriented development policies.
So much of the apparatus of the common institutions, the
employment provided by them, and their expenditures were
concentrated in Kenya that Tanzania and Uganda were firmly of
the belief that they operated mainly for the benefit of
Kenya. Increasing attention was given to the absence of any
instruments to regulate the operation of the common market,
other than the fiscal transfers through the Distributable
Pool. These transfers were not large enough to convince
Uganda and Tanzania that they resulted in an acceptable
distribution of the benefits of the common market and common
services. To the other members the arrangements still seemed
to contribute to the growing economic dominance of Kenya.

III THE KAMPALA-MBALE AGREEMENT

There was one instrument of policy already in existence
which, though devised for rather different purposes could be
used to affect the distribution of the benefits from the
common market. This was the industrial licensing system
which had been introduced in 1948 to attract industrial
investment by restricting competition with licensed firms,
but which had not been used to influence the location of
industry. Tanzania argued that the licensing system should

be used for this purpose, so as to achieve an equitable balance in the location of industry among the three countries. The so-called Kampala-Mbale Agreement of 1964-65, signed against the background of a threat by Tanzania to withdraw from the common market, had the following components: (a) a shift in the location of production by a number of firms which produced in two or more of the countries; (b) quotas on inter-territorial trade to encourage production in each country for its own domestic market; (c) the allocation of certain major industries to a particular country when they were set up; (d) an increase in sales from a country in deficit in inter-territorial trade to a country in surplus; (e) a system of inducements and allocations to secure an equitable distribution between the countries of future industrial development. Some measures under (a) were taken, but the constructive and longer term measures under (c) and (e), which culd have created a planned common market which achieved an acceptable and equitable location of development, were never put into effect. Before enough time had passed for the details of such measures to be worked out severe restrictions began to be imposed in inter-territorial trade, and the prospect of a collapse of the common arrangements emerged.

This was the background to the establishment of the commission of ministers of the three countries, meeting under an independent chairman, which produced the report on which the 1967 Treaty for East African Co-operation was based.

IV ECONOMIC INSTRUMENTS OF THE TREATY FOR EAST AFRICAN CO-OPERATION

The Treaty is a complex document in which the different components are inter-related, and the extent to which the Treaty was designed to work as a whole must not be forgotten. Nevertheless, it is helpful to identify some major economic instruments devised for the regulation of the Community.

The purpose of the regulatory instruments was to achieve, in the words of the Treaty, "accelerated, harmonious and balanced development and sustained expansion of economic activities the benefits whereof shall be equitably shared". The "planning" solution of the Kampala Agreement for achieving an acceptable location of industry was not revived.

Instead, a number of other instruments were created to ensure that the benefits of co-operation were "equitably shared". One instrument was the transfer tax which could be levied by a Partner State which was in overall deficit in inter-state trade against particular products from another Partner State with which it was in deficit. The pattern of inter-state trade at the time of the Treaty was such as under the rules to allow Tanzania to impose transfer taxes against Kenya and Uganda, and Uganda to impose them against Kenya. Kenya, being in surplus in inter-state trade, could not impose transfer taxes. The minimum rate of transfer tax was set at 50 per cent of the external tariff for the product in question. The introduction of transfer taxes was a retreat from the full common market as it enabled, for instance, Tanzania to protect certain industries against competition from Kenya.

Another new instrument for pursuing the policy of an "equitable distribution" was the East African Development Bank. The Bank was to be financed in equal amounts by the Partner States, with the expectation that further funds would be obtained from outside sources. It was to promote industrial development, give priority to the relatively less industrially developed partner states, and finance projects which would make the economies of the three states more complementary. It was required by its Charter to favour Tanzania and Uganda by investing 38-3/4 per cent of its resources in each of them, and only 22-1/2 per cent in Kenya.

Finally, the use of the common services as an instrument of distribution policy must be noted. It was not that the managements of the services were to be directed deliberately to favour the less-developed states, in the structure of the railway tariff, for instance. Indeed, the Treaty attempts to protect the managements from pressures by governments to provide non-remunerative services. But cross-subsidization between different parts of the services and between different regions was not prohibited, and this was a consideration in persuading at least one of the countries to accept the "package" presented in the Treaty. There was also to be a shift in the location of the headquarters of some services, so that they, with their attendant employment and expenditures, were not all located in Kenya. The headquarters of the new Community itself was to be located in Tanzania.

127

It was evident from the fact of the collapse of the Community that the instruments of economic policy created by the Treaty were ineffective: they did not work in a way that persuaded the members that continued co-operation was worthwhile. But that is to do with the partner states' perception of the benefits of co-operation, a matter further considered below, and does not necessarily mean that the instruments established by the Treaty were inappropriate for their purpose. It is worth, therefore, looking in a little more detail at the three policy instruments already described.

Transfer Tax

The transfer tax is sometimes seen as a device for encouraging the duplication of industries within East Africa, whereas the rationale of the common market was to avoid such duplication and to enable industries to enjoy economies of scale resulting from access to the whole East African market. But this criticism seems to derive from a misunderstanding, even though in practice it may be true that uneconomic duplication took place -- the multiplication of steel-mills has been given as an example. The rationale of the transfer tax system was that it would allow Tanzania and Uganda temporarily to protect from Kenyan competition industries which could operate efficiently on a scale provided by their national markets. For these industries, the encouragement of duplication was the whole purpose of the transfer tax, not an unwelcome and unintended side-effect. There were other, large scale, industries the location of which would not, according to this rationalization of the system, be affected by transfer taxes, because only a single plant would be economic for the whole of East Africa. Herein, however, lies the weakness of the rationalization: the distinction between the two types of industry is nothing like so clear cut as the rationalization presumes, and if sufficient incentives are provided, industries with important economies of scale could be duplicated to serve national markets at high cost. Such inefficient duplication cannot be blamed on the transfer tax. As formal fiscal incentives differed little between the Partner States it is probable that practices incompatible with the Treaty, including discriminatory purchasing by state trading corporations (see below) and quantitative restrictions on imports, were the major cause of inefficient duplication of industries, and that the transfer tax was never really given a fair trial.

East African Development Bank

The effectiveness of the East African Development Bank as an equalizing device may be questioned because of the limited scale of its activities. By the end of 1975 its investments in total were little more than twice the original contributions of the Partner States. On average the annual commitment of funds by the Bank accounted for no more than 4 per cent of industrial investment in the Partner States. It may be that a much larger scale of operations was expected by the less-developed Partner States when they agreed to the constitution of the Bank. But the Bank did rapidly achieve the prescribed distribution of its investments between the Partner States (until its activities in Uganda were disrupted by political developments) and, is possible that if the Community as a whole had proved a success outside finance would have become available to enable the scale of Bank operations to increase substantially. However, the most important role of the Bank could be seen as to act as a catalyst for complementary industrial development rather than to undertake a major part of industrial investment itself. And in that respect there is certainly reason to question its effectiveness. The projects in which the Bank invested (textiles, sugar, paper, tyres, cement, for example) do not appear particularly relevant to the aim of making the economies of the Partner States more complementary. It would have been difficult for the Bank alone to pursue this aim. It could have done so if agreements had existed between the Partner States on a pattern of industrial specialization into which the Bank's investments would fit. But regional planning, which is discussed later, did not get very far during the life of the Community.

Common Services

The further mechanism in the Treaty for distributing the gains from co-operation more equally was the relocation of the headquarters of the common services, which was combined with some decentralization of their operations. Perhaps too much was expected from these changes, because the greater part of the local expenditures made by the services, and of the employment provided by them, continued to benefit Kenya. The main activities of the services continued to be in Kenya in consequence of her higher level of development, as well as of geographical factors, and a change in the distribution could only occur in the longer run with relatively greater economic growth in Tanzania and Uganda.

These three instruments for regulating the distribution of the benefits of co-operation appear, therefore, to have been appropriate to their purpose. Their failings were rather in strength and speed. In any case, there were many other influences on the operation of the Community which must be taken into account in assessing the affects of the regutory devices of the Treaty.

V. OTHER ISSUES IN THE FUNCTIONING OF THE COMMUNITY

Community Government

The Treaty established a complicated institutional structure to administer and control the Community. In addition to a secretariat there were a number of Councils, at which discussions took place between representatives of the Partner States, and an East African Minister and Assistant Minister for each Partner State. Ultimate control rested with the Authority composed of the three Presidents. Although in the end the structure proved powerless to ensure the survival of the Community, its effectiveness should not be judged by the experience of the period following the coup which took place in Uganda in January, 1971. It can be objected that the system relied too much on harmonious relations between the Presidents, and that control of the Community collapsed when relations became bad, and the source of initiative for the continuation and development of cooperation died. It is also true that even during the first few years the existence of the Authority seemed to deprive lower levels in the administration of the Community of initiative and of willingness to seek solutions to issues between the Partner States by compromise. The structure of control encouraged the pursuit of national interests and discouraged compromise, because there was always the Authority to reach an agreement in the end. And in the first three years of the Community's existence it did reach agreement, and although the history of the Community even before the Uganda coup can be read as a lurch from crisis to crisis, the Authority was adept at resolving crises.

There is something to be said for the view that a system which encouraged compromise at a lower level - ministerial rather than Presidential, and among officials - would have made the relations between the Partner States less crisis-prone, and the Community machinery of cooperation to run more smoothly. There is also something to be said for the view that the Secretary-General and the secretariat had too limited powers with all decisions requiring the specific agreement of the Partner States. However, it is certain that at the time the Treaty was signed, the Partner States would have been unwilling to allow any delegation of powers to the secretariat of the Community. The importance of sovereignty in the first flush of independence would have prevented any delegation of powers, and gives credence to the view that arrangements which require a surrender of sovereignty if they are to work efficiently - even if it goes no further than a commitment to consultation before decisions are taken - are exceptionally difficult for new nations.

Unanimous or majority rule is a related issue. The Partner States did not, and certainly would not have agreed to action by majority decision. In a community of thre members majority rule is in any case difficult because of the risk that one country may find itself repeatedly in a minority of one. But even in a larger community it is almost inconceivable that majority rule would have been acceptable, and unanimity would have been even more difficult to achieve in a larger grouping. The Treaty could certainly have been adapted for a larger Community, but it is probably true that only Zambia was ever a serious applicant, so a solution to the issue of unanimity or majority rule could hardly have been found in that direction.

Transport Issues

A number of issues concerning transport, and the related issue of tourism, caused tensions between the Partner States.

131

The Kenya tourist industry benefitted from access to the game parks of northern Tanzania. They were generally included in a circuit for Nairobi-based tourists, using Kenya vehicles. Although payments were obviously made for the use of Tanzania's hotels and game parks, and for other goods and services, nonetheless it was strongly contended by Tanzania that she received only minor benefits from the traffic. Geographical convenience made northern Tanzania a natural part of a Nairobi-based tour, and at the time it would have been implausible to expect a cross-border tour to be based anywhere else. Arusha could have been an alternative base, but not until there had been a very substantial expansion in the infra-structure for tourism, and a change in Tanzania's somewhat ambivalent attitude towards the industry. Tourism is an industry where a redistribution of the benefits rather than a relocation of activities was the way to maximize total benefits and improve their distribution. A great share for Tanzania would have required an agreement permitting discriminatory charges and other measures, and such arrangements could have been brought under the Treaty. The closure of the border and the disappearance of cross-border tourism with the collapse of the Community, must have reduced the total benefits of tourism. Although it has stimulated Tanzania's interest in tourism, and she may be gaining more from tourism than in the past, the gains could have been greater still from cross-border tourism with an equitable distribution of the benefits.

A substantial road traffic developed between Kenya and Zambia, crossing Tanzania. The benefits of the trade accrued to Kenya whereas it imposed costs on Tanzania from the use of Tanzanian roads by heavy vehicles. Tension arose between Kenya and Tanzania over this issue. Competition between road and rail was also a cause of tension. It was thought by some that the growth of road transport in Kenya was to the benefit of private business in Kenya at the expense of the jointly-owned public railway. In fact, the issue was a good deal more complicated than that, competition between road and rail being a matter of long standing in East Africa. Large investments in road vehicles for the carriage of petroleum products had been made by private interests in Kenya, and the argument just reported was largely directed at that, but as it happens these investments had been made at a time when large investments in railway rolling stock would also have been needed if the railway was to handle the traffic. In any case, the opening of a publicly-owned pipe line from the coast to Nairobi to carry petroleum products, displacing both road and rail, suggests that a juxtaposition of private and public transport interests was too simple an interpretation of the issue. Nevertheless, the simple interpretation had some effect in souring relations between Kenya and Tanzania, and Tanzania eventually closed the border to Kenya's heavy vehicles, even before the general border closure.

The omission from the Treaty of detailed provisions for road transport followed naturally from the fact that it did not exist as a common service. The issues arising could nevertheless have been dealt with under the Treaty. The costs imposed by the use of Tanzanion roads by heavy vehicles from Kenya could have been dealt with by the levying of appropriately heavy charges, so long as the charges did not formally discriminate in favour of Tanzanian vehicles. The issues of road-rail competition were discussed in the Communications Council, one of the Community Institutions established by the Treaty, but much more needed to be done to produce and implement a plan for the coordinated development of surface transport throughout East Africa. Without it, transport issues were a disruptive influence on the Community.

State Trading

Transport coordination was an old issue left unsettled by the Treaty in which the absence of a settlement led to strains between the Partner States. A new issue of the same kind was that of state trading, which came into prominence soon after the Treaty was signed. The Treaty was implicitly written for a common market of market economies, in which marketing decisions were based on prices. The transfer taxes were designed to protect national industries while preserving a preference for the goods of other Partner States over goods from outside East Africa. The whole system was based on the assumption that the transfer tax and the external tariff would establish certain price relationships, and that purchasing decisions would be based on those prices. This assumption became rapidly out of date with the growth of state trading in the Partner States. State trading corporations, with a monopoly of purchasing for distribution, could be directed and might be expected even without direction to discriminate in favour of domestic suppliers, and there was evidence that this was occurring. Rules were drawn up for the regulation of state trading, though they would have been difficult but not impossible to enforce. It must be said, however, that state trading could have been turned into an integrating rather than a disintegrating device if it had been able to operate within a system of, and as an instrument for the implementation of, inter-state planning.

Planning

It might be argued that the relevance of inter-state planning in an integration scheme of developing countries is enhanced by the extent to which industrial development is undertaken with foreign capital, and in particular by transnational corporations. In a largely laissez faire scheme, including a scheme where the market is rigged by a device such as the transfer tax, even if fiscal incentives are harmonized, the members will be competing for the favour of foreign firms, and consequently their bargaining power will be drastically reduced. There will be duplication of investments which will dissipate the gains, and the gains in any case will go mainly to the foreign enterprise. This possibility provides a further argument for inter-state planning to reinforce cooperation, but its relevance to East Africa is a good deal diminished by the apparently unwelcoming face at times presented by Tanzania to foreign enterprises. However, the development of manufacturing in Kenya by transnationals led some to the view that by importing from Kenya, Tanzania was allowing herself to be exploited by these concerns.

It would be too easy, in fact, to blame the absence of planning for the failure to solve these problems and, indeed, the whole issue of the distribution of the benefits of cooperation. Planning had a place in the Treaty where provision was made for an Economic Consultative and Planning Council, and a committee of officials, the East African Committee of Planners, was set up. Planning was not simply something the framers of the Treaty forgot. Of course, the Treaty could have given a central role to planning, and established a planning instead of a pricing mechanism to deal with the distribution of industry. But it is certain, particularly as it was so soon after the failure of the Kampala Agreement on the allocation of industries, that a planning system would not have been accepted.   There would have been no treaty signed if that had been its central feature. Despite discussions within the Community institutions, planning proposals never came anywhere near to implementation.   If planning, particularly of the development of industry, is a sine qua non of successful regional integration, as some authorities believe, the failure to undertake such planning was obviously a major cause of the collapse of the Community. But it may be that successful regional planning requires such a high degree of harmony between the member states that, if the conditions for success exist, many of the problems planning is required to solve would not have arisen.

Balance of Payments Problems

Another issue which was neither ignored in the Treaty nor given sufficient importance, concerns the balance of payments and foreign exchange problems of the Partner States. The issue was to become more serious and express itself in ways which it may be guessed were not fully foreseen at the time the Treaty was drawn up.

The settlement of net indebtedness arising from interstate transactions had in effect to be in foreign exchange. There was a provision for the extension of credit by a state in surplus in inter-state trade to one in deficit, but the maximum credit was relatively small, and the scheme was in fact never brought into use, though there may have been informal inter-state lending. The provisions of the Treaty were to the advantage of Kenya, which relied on a surplus in inter-state trade to balance a significant part of her deficit in external trade.   It is unlikely that Kenya would have accepted a scheme which provided for balances to be inconvertible and which did not allow her to earn foreign exchange from inter-state trade, given that she had accepted discrimination against herself in the form of the transfer tax and the investment allocations of the EADB, and given the lower free market rates of Tanzania and Uganda Shillings. But the resulting large foreign exchange costs of inter-state settlements had very serious consequences.

Foreign exchange scarcity, though it was already a problem, suddenly became of major importance with the rise in oil prices, and to save foreign exchange became a major preoccupation of governments. It would have been consistent with a commitment to East African cooperation if inter-state transactions had been immune from restrictions. But that was not to be, and in the application of restrictions to imports there was no discrimination in favour of imports from other Partner States.

A perhaps unforeseen effect of foreign exchange scarcity, which played an important part in the collapse of the Community Institutions and in souring the atmosphere in the last years of their existence, was the imposition of restrictions on the transfer of funds from the regions to the headquarters of the common services. It is unnecessary to rehearse the sorry tale of squabbles and recriminations, and the charges and counter-charges of responsibility for the failure to transfer funds. The blame cannot be entirely attributed to the desire to save foreign exchange, for, if the affairs of the common services had been in good order it would have been more difficult for payments to be stopped on exchange control grounds. But the fact is that the common services, already in a state of disarray, were fundamentally disrupted by the drying-up of the flow of funds to headquarters, where lay the responsibility for large expenditures, including the purchase of equipment and loan charges. This disruption in the financial operation of the services led directly to their effective dissolution as common institutions and to the collapse of a major part of the structure of the Community.

Amin

The founders of the Community could not have been expected to legislate against the appearance of General Amin, and his seizure of power is one of the matters which was not amenable to settlement in advance by Treaty. Nevertheless, the crucial position of the Authority, to which reference has already been made, raises again the question of whether a different structure of control would have been less sensitive to such events. The Authority did not meet after Amin came to power in Uganda, although other initial disruption the essential business was conducted by obtaining the agreement of the members individually. But the atmosphere was not conducive to smooth operation of the Community, let alone to that progressive extension of cooperation which some have seen as necessary for success. Uganda ceased to be an effective participant in Community discussions and the balance of the Community's tripartite structure disappeared.

Ideology

Nor is it easy to see that the Treaty could have done anything about the growing ideological division between "capitalist" Kenya and "socialist" Tanzania, if these short-hand terms may be allowed to represent the positions of the two governments. When there were all the other disruptive influences at work, the different ideologies of the governments of Kenya and Tanzania certainly made cooperation increasingly difficult, particularly as they were used from time to time as pegs on which to hang mutual political abuse. However, too much can perhaps be made of this cause of dissension as the reason for the inevitable collapse of the Community. After all, procedures for dealing with the problems created by the establishment of state monopoly trading corporations had been devised by the Community Secretariat, though they had not been implemented. Certainly, determined proseletization of one side by the other could make cooperation impossible. But it would be a conclusion of despair that mutually beneficial economic cooperation requires a close similarity of social and political outlook. And it must be emphasized that the fundamental assumption on which the Treaty was based was that integration was a "positive sum game" from which all could benefit, particularly in the longer run when the volume of mutually beneficial intra-Community trade had expanded. And here, perhaps, we come to the heart of the matter. As time went on the Partner States increasingly behaved as if they believed it was in fact a "zero sum game", or even a "negative sum game".

Changing Perceptions

There was, it must be admitted, some justification for such a belief, to an extent indeed because of the way the Partner States had behaved. The benefits from the common market began to disappear with the duplication of industries. The benefits of the common services were dissipated in inefficiences and financial difficulties. With increased road competition on the Mambosa-Nairobi rail route, and with extra rail traffic in Tanzania arising from the construction of the

137

Tanzania-Zambia railway (itself established as a separate entity from East African Railways) the pattern of cross-subsidization within the railway system shifted, and Tanzania appeared to be benefitting less than before from the joint system. The establishment of TAZARA outside the Community was a sign of less than wholehearted commitment in Tanzania, and the increase in imports from China under the agreement for financing the local costs of the railway, Tanzania having failed to obtain support from Western donors or international institutions, had an adverse effect on inter-state trade.

But even more important than the objective situation was the perception of the Partner States about the costs and benefits of the system. If the perception of the partners is that there are gains for all, then the bargaining is about how much better-off each shall be, and only if one partner is pushed to the limit will it be worth its while to withdraw. Even where it is such a positive-sum game, however, the perceptions of the partners may be inconsistent. One partner may think it is not receiving enough of the benefit, at a time when another partner thinks it has itself been pushed to near the limit. There is reason to think that the perceptions of Tanzania and Kenya, respectively, were something like this when the Treaty was signed. It is doubtful if Kenya would have accepted a more unfavourable bargain. It would be a mistake to think that at the signing of the Treaty the Kenya ministers and officials were chortling at the thought that they had made a very advantageous deal. Yet Tanzania may have felt that the Treaty gave her little more than the minimum she was prepared to accept, and developments in the succeeding years may have made her even less satisfied.

Although the definition and the measurement of the "gap" between the levels of development in Kenya and Tanzania are fraught with difficulties, which are enhanced by the different ends of "capitalist" and "socialist" societies, the gap evidently did not narrow and probably increased in the perceptions of both Tanzania and Kenya, despite the growth of industry in Tanzania. Given that the growth of the Kenya economy was to be a significant extent the consequences of the welcome it gave to foreign investors, a route to development of which Tanzania to say the least was wary, the equalizing mechanisms of the Treaty were attempting to swim against a strongly flowing stream. That inequality was perceived to remain or increase led to a loss of interest in cooperation, because of hubris in Kenya, where the ill effects of a loss of exports to Tanzania and Zambia may have been greatly underestimated, being concealed by the boom in the price of coffee, and of despair in Tanzania at cooperation with Kenya as a route to development. All in all, there was a change in the perceived benefits of continued cooperation and in the perceived costs of dissolution. Perceived as a zero- or negative-sum game the Community had no future, even though the perceptions may have been erroneous.

Other Influences

Interest in East African cooperation was crumbling also for other reasons. Reference has already been made to the coup in Uganda as disrupting relations between Tanzania and Uganda. In addition, the focus of political interest in Tanzania moved towards the south. The future of Zimbabwe, and Tanzania's position as a Front Line State, attracted political attention at the highest levels and, it may be suspected, diminished the concern with the strengthening of East African relations. If this is so, it would be one reason why the crisis-solving function of the Authority ceased to be effective.

This discussion has been in terms of the interests and benefits of the Partner States, but the states are not monolithic and within them there are different interests which would be effected differently by the success or by the failure of cooperation between the states. A full understanding of the brief history of the Community is impossible without an understanding of how that history was both affected by and affected these various interests. It is a matter very difficult to research, and largely unresearched, but it is of importance. And much the same must be said about external interests - foreign governments, transnational corporations, international institutions.

VI. QUESTIONS

It has already been remarked that there was no single cause of the death of the East African Community, no simple inadequacy in the regulating instruments, but rather a multiplicity of ailments, each of which by itself could have been survived, but which together were too much for the weakened body to bear. Nor can it be said that the Community was killed: rather it faded and died from a lack of interest in keeping it alive, though not without a nudge or two along the road to the grave, and not without some squabbles between the heirs to the estate. In short, the political will was lacking in the Partner States to keep the Community in being.

Spilt milk is, notoriously, not worth crying over. However, it may be worthwhile to examine the reasons for the spillage, particularly if to do so will help to prevent a similar waste in the future. It is perhaps surprising that the death of the Community has not killed the apparent interest in regional integration schemes of varying degrees among developing countries, in Africa and elsewhere. There are still schemes in various stages of development in different parts of the world. Certainly the members of new schemes elsewhere would not have the history of disagreement which in East Africa began with the unregulated common market of colonial times. A well-designed new scheme which fully met each member's perception of the costs and benefits, if such a scheme could be designed, would not have the tensions created by years of controversy. On the other hand, most groupings lack what might be expected to be the valuable lubricants for smoothly working cooperation of common languages, as with English and Swahili in East Africa, and the common educational background provided by Makerere for some politicians and for many of the generation of civil servants who took over the administration of all three East African countries at independence. ECOWAS (the Economic Community of West African States) and the proposed preferential trading area for which 16 Eastern and Southern African countries signed a treaty of intent in March, 1978, and which was seen as a first step in a process of regional integration, are two schemes that might benefit from the lessons of the East African Community.

It is not easy to summarize the lessons for the planners of other schemes, so that they can be learned by rote. Perhaps the best approach is to list some of the questions about the requirements for successful regional integration that are suggested by a study of the Community's history:

1. Is it necessary only that all members of the scheme should benefit, or must they benefit equally, or must the poorer or less developed members gain most, or must even the gap between the members in their wealth and level of development actually narrow over time? The last is a very strong requirement, because it is perfectly possible for the gap to widen, even though the integration arrangements themselves have a strong equalizing element.

2. Is there a limit to the difference in levels of development and "economic size" of members of a grouping beyond which integration cannot work? Are giants and pygmies incompatible cohabitants?

3. Are members willing to take a longer-term view, and to see the benefits from cooperation grow with the growth of trade between them, or do their assessments inevitably have a short horizon within which transactions between them, and hence the benefits of cooperation, are likely to be small?

4. If there are gains from the scheme for the members as a whole and for every member individually, can it be ensured that they all perceive the benefit, and do not have incompatible perceptions of the distribution of the benefits?

5. Are the members prepared to agree on a common system of fiscal incentives to encourage an acceptable distribution of investment between them and to prevent the competitive offering of concessions to investors?

6. Is it possible for the operation of the scheme to be insulated from the effects of foreign exchange scarcity in the member countries?

7. Is a substantial degree of regional planning over such matters as the location of new industries and the pattern of industrial specialization essential to achieve an acceptable distribution of the benefits of integration?

8. If so, are the member countries prepared to accept the

constraints imposed on them by such planning?

9. How does such planning cope with strong preferences by potential investors about the location of production?

10. Is a complex or "package" scheme, embracing different fields of cooperation, as in East Africa, where some parts of the scheme may be of particular benefit to some member(s), and other parts to others, most likely to lead to all members perceiving that there are benefits from membership?

11. Would a less comprehensive scheme, in which areas of cooperation with the greatest potential for conflict were excluded, be more viable?

12. Would "functionally specific" arrangements of limited scope be the best bet?

13. Would provisions in the Treaty for a common agricultural policy have been a cohesive influence in the community? Is it important to include agriculture in integration arrangements for countries where it is the major economic activity?

14. Is a broadly similar ideology in the member countries essential for success?

15. Is continuing political harmony between the states essential and must it go beyond the minimum of good will without which cooperation would be impossible?

16. Must the members be willing to surrender sovereignty to the extent of allowing decisions to be reached by majority vote?

17. Must the members be prepared to delegate substantial powers to the bureaucracy of the scheme?

18. Can a scheme be protected from the effect of a wavering commitment to integration of the highest levels in one or more of the Partner States?

19. Is the absence of political rewards at the regional

level likely to reduce the political will and interest in integration below the minimum necessary for success?

20. What is the balance of influence within each country and what interests will be harmed or benefitted by the progress of integration?

21. What external influences are at work and which favour and which oppose integration?

22. Are the expected gains from industrialization to serve a protected regional market great enough to make it worthwhile surmounting the difficulties, given the possibilities for manufacturing for extra-regional export, including export to developed countries through the medium of multinational corporations? The expectation will differ from country to country according to the size of its domestic market and its competitive ability in international markets. A firmly affirmative answer from every member would probably be necessary if a grouping were to have strong prospect of success.

The answers to at least some of these questions might seem obvious, but the implications of such answers have not always been taken into account in regional integration proposals. And unless the founders of regional integration schemes in developing countries are satisfied with their answers to all these questions their efforts may be described, in Dr. Johnson's words on the second marriage of a man whose first had been unhappy, as the triumph of hope over experience.

Chapter VI

Footnotes

1. This chapter is based on two of the author's previous publications: _Economic Integration: The East African Experience_, (London: Heinemann, 1975), and "The End of the East African Community: What are the Lessons for Regional Integration Schemes?", _Journal of Common Market Studies_, (September, 1979).

CHAPTER VII

Who Killed Cock Robin? An Analysis of
Perceptions Concerning the Breakup
of the East African Community

Christian P. Potholm

COCK ROBIN

Who killed Cock Robin?
I, said the Sparrow,
With my bow and arrow,
I killed Cock Robin.

Who saw him die?
I, said the Fly,
With my little eye,
I saw him die.

Who caught his blood?
I, said the Fish,
With my little dish
I caught his blood.

Who'll make the shroud?
I, said the Beetle,
With my thread and needle
I'll make the shroud.

Who'll dig his grave?
I, said the Owl,
With my pick and shovel,
I'll dig his grave.

Who'll be the parson?
I, said the Rook,
With my little book,
I'll be the parson.

. . . .

Who'll toll the bell?
I, said the Bull,
Because I can pull,
I'll toll the bell.

All the birds of the air
Fell a-sighing and a-sobbing,
When they heard the bell toll
For poor Cock Robin.

146

Unlike the candor expressed in the poem, those connected with the breakup of the East African Community have been slow to accept responsibility for it. Indeed, there are almost as many theories as to who killed cock robin as there are participants. And, although most observers agree that there were a number of ingredients which were present in the situation surrounding the breakup, few can agree as to which were decisive in the demise of the Community.(1)

In addition to scholarly interest in the breakup itself, and the long-term implications for Kenya, Uganda and Tanzania, the breakup of the East African Community in 1977 following a decade of operation has also raised numerous questions about the nature of regional cooperation in Africa and suggests that many earlier hypotheses concerning the desirability of economic rather than political grouping have been incorrect, particularly with regard to the notion that economic variables would necessarily override political concerns.

In this chapter, I am not attempting to detail the breakup of the Community nor am I endeavoring - except tangentially - to ascribe "blame" for that breakup.(2) Nor will I be attempting to duplicate the existing historical accounts of the Community.(3) Instead, in the words of Roberts Wohlstetter, I shall be endeavoring to display "a willingness to play with material from different angles...in the context of unpopular as well as popular hypotheses,"(4) from the points of view provided by both participants as well as local observers.

In other words, I am primarily interested here in examining the perceptions - and misperceptions - of those who were a part of the Community, those who subsequently took over responsibility for many of its functions and those who observed its decay over time.(5) This is a complex process and in a short work, I can only hope to point in the direction of some preceptional patterns which may or may not be correlated to specific groups of actors. And my judgements about the accuracy and inaccuracy of the decision-makers' perceptions are made in the context of essential fluidity and indeed existential processes for:

The evidence available to decision-makers is

almost always very ambiguous since accurate clues to others' intentions are surrounded by 'noise' and deception. In most cases, no matter how long, deeply and 'objectively' the evidence is analyzed, people can differ in their interpretations, and there are no general rules to indicate who is correct.(6)

In my search for both patterns of perceptions and correlations within and among actor-groups, we must also take into account the powerful gravitational pulls exerted by bureaucratic as well as national and ethnic locations for, as Graham Allison has so aptly put it, "where you stand depends on where you sit."(7) In the East African context, one is constantly struck by the divergent views of society, economics and politics held, not only by the citizens and government officials of Tanzania, Uganda and Kenya but by the international civil servants from those countries as well. As a result, in the sections which follow I make no effort to explain whatever level of individual cognitive distortion results from this positional extrapolation except to try to put it in its proper perceptional pattern. In other words, I shall often attempt to explain the origins of the perceptional pattern in general without specific reference to individual cognitive distortion or perspicacious transmission.

Perceptional Pattern #1: Ideology Influenced the Outcome

A number of observers and participants have argued that the East African Community was "destined" to fail once the three member states moved in widely different ideological directions: Kenya into an Africanized version of international capitalism (but with some socio-statist elements), Tanzania into Ujamaa socialism and Uganda moving from a mixed to a proto-socialist economy and then to a praetorian despotic one.

This view was expressed by a number of government officials who stated that the Community "could not continue to work" as these ideological differences developed. Interestingly enough, many who held this view did not place the blame on tribal or even national attachments. Their assessment was apparently based less on a national-unit impulse than on the ideological assessments and mind sets. In other words, Tanzanian officials who saw the government and private sector intermeshing through KENATCO to give Kenya truckers an economic advantage stressed that what troubled them was not simply Kenyan truckers taking business from Tanzanian railroads but rather, Kenyan entrepreneurs ("capitalists") taking profits from Tanzanian peasants by using their roads.(8)

It is intriguing to trace this strand in previous Tanzanian attitudes toward infrastructural alternatives with regard to Zambia. The original World Bank study indicated that economically (and in terms of employment possibilities) an all-weather road from Dar es Salaam to Lusaka was preferable to a railroad. Among the various reasons Tanzanians gave for preferring the Chinese-built TanZam railroad was that railroads were in and of themselves "more" socialistic.(9)

For those Kenyans who owned - or operated - trucks, Tanzanian concern over road use and "exploitation" seemed to make little sense for they tended to regard the end result; i.e., X number of goods at Y price delivered to Z location as far more important than whether a particular road got more use than another. That is to say, to them, how the goods got from point A to point B and the fact that whoever got them there made a profit were far less relevant than the alternative. To them, it was simply a question of the availability of a good versus its unavailability.

For Nyerere and numerous Tanzanian government officials, the unwillingness of Kenya to agree to compensate them for the initial (and continuing) Kenyan economic advantages were also seen in ideological terms. After all, Nyerere had offered to hold back Tanganyikan independence until Kenya "caught up" politically. Was it asking too much for Kenya to now assist Tanzania in catching up economically? Extrapolating the principles of Ujamaa socialism to the national and international level clearly meant that one should expect Kenya to do just that. Extrapolating Kenya's competitive capitalism to the international level, however, meant that without compensating mechanisms a crude form of social Darwinism had developed and it would be intolerable to allow that to continue.(10)

I shall be examining this element in greater detail in

149

the section on economic realities but it should be pointed out with regard to those who stress the efficacy of ideological differences that one could argue that many holders of this perception often seem to confuse the impact of the nature of a power relationship with ideological efficacy.(11)

Perceptional Pattern #2: The Critical Failure of Political Leadership

If a number of government officials tend to blame the breakup of the Community on ideological (or at least extrapolated national operational attitudes) grounds, many former officials disagree strongly with this perception. For many Community technocrats, even up to the highest levels (and if the conversations were kept off the record, even including those who subsequently found employment with one of the governments in question), the blame clearly should be placed on the shoulders of the three presidents, Jomo Kenyatta, Julius Nyerere and Idi Amin.

For these actors, it was not simply a matter of the three not agreeing as to the future direction of the Community. Rather, it was that the three presidents simply failed to focus on the problem until the Community had been completely enervated. Jomo Kenyatta was preoccupied with internal dissention, keeping the economy stable and international investment flowing (and less charitably to make sure that The Family and Kikuyu nepotism did not diminish). Idi Amin was preoccupied both with staying alive and purging Ugandan society as well as with international activity and staying in the African spotlight.(12)

For his part, it can probably be argued that of all three, Julius Nyerere was personally most interested in the problem but he too, was intensely preoccupied during the disintegration of the Community. The serious, even critical problems with the Ujamaa village program were only a part of it. Increasingly during the 1970's Nyerere had his attention drawn, not to East Africa but to the South, to Zambia and Mozambique, and following the successful independence of the latter, to the questions of the liberation of Zimbabwe, Namibia and the changing political configurations of southern Africa. For all the frustration inherent in that situation, there can be little doubt that Nyerere found the game and the potential prizes (as well as potential disasters) far more interesting and personally engaging than who got what share of what revenues from what common services.

Thus, many Community technocrats argue, in the absence of general pro-Community sentiment and presidential interest, their positions were undercut by the political statements of individuals in Kenya and Tanzania and indeed often by the press in both countries. The end result was that the problems of the Community escalated beyond the ability of bureaucrats, no matter how well intentioned, to cope with them. Lack of presidential interest, not any appropriate ideological handicap, then doomed the Community.

While this view clearly ascribes to the three presidents a freedom of action (i.e., to be involved in a subject at a time of their choosing) which they may or may not have enjoyed, certainly from a perceptional point of view, this view has a certain internal consistency. Moreover, the widespread nature of its holding is explained in terms of the situational progression. And, in fact, the various national ministries represented on the Councils may well have some bureaucratic and political reasons for taking a "national" stance and thereby bump the issue back to the presidents' purview.

As Robert Jarvis has written, "The way people perceive data is influenced not only by their cognitive structure and theories about other actors but also by what they are concerned with at the time they receive the information."(13) Thus, the Community officials who had often joined the Community in its earlier, expansive phase had a sense that the Community was important to the highest office-holders in the three countries. As long as the Community flourished, they were content to have the political leaders occupied elsewhere, but as the Community began to disintegrate, their sense of urgency was twofold: what would happen to the Community, what would happen to themselves and their jobs. Therefore, it was not surprising that they looked more and more intently to the presidents for guidance and toward the end to play the role of a deux ex machina. When this was not forthcoming, it certainly heightened their frustration and intensified their perceptions as to the importance of presidential attention.

Perceptional Pattern #3:   Economic Realities
Could Not Be Denied

Another persistent perceptional pattern which has been advanced as explaining the breakup of the Community revolves around the so-called "economic realities."   While a number of observers and participants blurred this explanation with portions of the ideological pattern, it does seem that it can stand alone and, indeed, has been so expressed.

Kenya, as the wealthiest partner to begin with, the one with the largest internal market and the most highly developed industrial and commercial sectors, dominated Tanzania and Uganda. Kenya not only began with these advantages, she built on them during the 10 years of the Community. Her success - at least at measured by trade - was achieved, in part, at the expense of the other two countries.

Certainly this dimension was related in part to the Kenyan government's espousal of a modified form of capitalism and both an image and substance which suggested foreign investment could be made easily and profitably and therefore had ideological overtones.   But one could well argue that those who hypothesize Kenya acting because of ideology to establish itself as the capitalist "subimperialistic" power in the area clearly differ with those who feel that economic realities provide a better explanation than either political inactivity or ideological forms.

Middle management people, from multinational corporations, Kenyan subsidiaries or independent Kenyan companies, state that the Community was doomed when Nyerere and others linked the continuation of the Community to the East African Common Market, holding the latter up as hostage to the former.(14)   In other words, whatever the Tanzanians and Ugandans may have wished, the 10 years of Community had witnessed (and surely not reversed) the economic patterns which endured because they were "the correct one."

Bankers and businessmen in Kenya, as well as managers within the international corporations which located in Kenya, put it simply. Uganda became an economic shambles. In their mind, no firm in its right mind would invest in Amin's

152

Uganda.(15) Tanzania, never terribly attractive from an investment point of view, became less so as Ujamaa socialism was applied more stringently.(16) And, with Tanzanian difficulties in coping with the cargo situation in Dar es Salaam after the opening of the TanZam railroad, getting goods in and out of the country became a serious problem.

Why go to the trouble to invest in Tanzania or Uganda when things were so much easier in Kenya? Who would choose to live in Dar es Salaam (or worse yet, Dodoma) or in post-Amin Kampala, they asked. Candidly, they argued it was as much a case of ease and relative efficiency as the bottom line on a balance sheet. International corporations chose to locate in Nairobi for a variety of reasons, only some of which had to do directly with the Kenyan government (or its efforts to get firms to locate there rather than in the other two members of the Community).

David Baldwin had argued elsewhere that if A "gets" B to do something B would have done anyway, that is not influence, let alone intervention; it is simply a confluence of interests.(17) Thus, the economic concentration in Kenya during the decade of the Community, they feel, is explained by the Kenyan government going along with what foreign investors wanted to do anyway. This is not to say that Kenya did not actively encourage that investment, even in those areas where existing treaties called for the location of certain industries in Tanzania or Uganda. But it is to say that the perception managers and investors alike had, was that by locating in Kenya they were doing what they wished, not what the government of Kenya wished.

Tanzanian businessmen, often after giving lip service to the ideological elements in their situation, expressed a desire to have a piece of the Kenyan economic action, not eliminate it, and they often suggested that they would prefer to operate in a similar situation (not just under a similar governmental philosophy). This pattern of perceptions is hardly surprising but it does suggest that at least some people saw the efforts to disperse wealth throughout the Community as not only a nuisance but also an unnecessary one.(18)

While one can hardly blame the businessman for wanting to conduct business, or indeed some governments from wanting to curtail or at least monitor that business, it does suggest that in some real sense, the economic and political realities were truly distorted by the end of the 1977's. Surprisingly enough, an example which was common to both those who believed in the ideological explanation and those who believed in the "economic realities" explanation was that of the tourist trade.

Nyerere and the TANU leadership had been at best ambivalent as to the question of the value of tourism, both agreed. Those favoring an ideological explanation either thought this was or was not a good thing depending on their mind set, but accepted it as a fact and as something which affected the ways in which tourists were treated in Tanzania. The "economic realities" point of view, however, used tourism to underscore their point. The World Bank and the Community had gone to great lengths, they argued, to help Tanzania out with tourism, including the Arusha development surrounding the Kilimanjaro airport. Tanzania, with its Serengeti plains and Ngorongoro crater, probably had the greatest concentration of game in the world. As of 1978, this attitude may well have begun to change in Tanzania for the country opened its borders to hunting (after Kenya closed its borders in 1977) and attempted to spur tourism to a greater degree than at any point in the previous decade.

Yet, by the time of the border closing on April 18, 1977, the vast majority of tourists came to Nairobi, visited one or more Kenyan game parks and then visited Tanzania by road, spending most of their funds in Kenya, leaving millions of dollars behind.(19) This might or might not be good for Tanzania and Kenya, depending on one's point of view and much of the funds spent might well pass out of Kenya to other destinations, but one cannot argue that A half million tourists can be highly motivated by ideological concerns. The vast majority are not coming to East Africa to make a political statement for or against socialism or capitalism. They couldn't care less about whether their visit benefitted X country or Y country. All they cared about was good food, good service and a worthwhile experience. This, the "economic realities" types argued, they got in Kenya and not in Tanzania.

Perceptional Pattern #4: Exogenous Forces Destroyed the Community

As might be expected in 1977-1978 in Africa, there were a number of participants and other individuals who blamed the breakup of the Community on the hostility of exogenous forces. The forces of "neocolonialism," it was assumed, wished to see the Community rent asunder, thereby reducing the power of an African entity. These forces were variously referred to as (1) the United States, (2) Great Britain, (3) various multinational corporations, (4) Western capitalism or (5) some combination of these.

This viewpoint was widely held among Kenyan and Tanzanian students, intellectuals and a variety of middle-level managers in various ministries (for example, the Vice President's office in Kenya). It did not seem to be held by high-level ministry officials, former officials of the Community or Kenyan entrepreneurial types.

The belief in exogenous forces was quite strong and seemed to be based on two different, but mutually influencing sets of perceptions. On the one hand, the general history of Africa since independence was cited to draw examples of exogenous intrusions: the overthrow of Kwame Nkrumah, armed intervention by Western forces in the Congo (and later Zaire), the Nigerian civil war and the presence of foreign troops, including the French, in key strategic locations and the general patterns of economic domination as seen in terms of trade, fluctuations of primary-product prices and both governmental and corporate intrusions. These had already occurred in the history of Africa. The Community, which had been "good" for East Africa was breaking up; ergo, the same forces hostile to African "advancement" were involved.

More interesting perhaps was the second set of perceptions which were prevalent during 1977 and 1978 in Kenya. Exogenous forces were responsible for the breakup of the Community because they wanted to weaken Kenya in particular. In particular, it was often expressed that the United States, by (then apparently) siding with Somalia in its clash with Ethiopia over the future of the Ogaden was jeopardizing the long-term interest of Kenya. This meant that the United States was prepared to sacrifice the interests of Kenya vis-

155

a-vis a future Somali reassertion of its claim to Kenya's old Northern Frontier District (NFD) either because (1) there was oil in Somalia, (2) Saudi Arabia had insisted that the United States support Somalia, (3) American strategic interests in the Horn were greater than their interests in Kenya.

While all of this may seem a bit extreme in light of subsequent events and certainly is a point of view with glaring internal inconsistencies (such as the interests of a wide range of American firms in Kenya, not in Somalia even if there were oil or natural gas to interest American oil companies).(20) Yet, at the time, Somalia was clamoring for arms, the Kenyans had forced down an Egyptian plane carrying arms and Kenya certainly felt itself surrounded by potentially hostile regimes.

Whether those who held these perceptions were correct or not is not really germane to the main thrust of this chapter. What is of considerable interest is the frequency with which the view was held. And of even more significance is the extent to which this view was not held by people closely associated with the day-to-day workings of the Community apparatus. The fact that the "dominant inference pattern"(21) of most of those closely associated with the functions of the Community objected to the exogenous-influence argument does not, of course, mean that it is incorrect, but it suggests that if the exogenous forces were actually more than peripherally involved, their degree of subtlety vis-a-vis Community officials would have been truly extraordinary.

Perceptional Pattern #5: Changing Times Undercut the EAC

A number of observers were unwilling to give credit or cast blame in only one direction. This is very much the view of a number of scholars, such as Richard Fredland.(22) In their view, a number of factors came into play over time and these had a cumulative effect on the Community which could not be denied except by vigorous action at the presidential level, action which was not forthcoming.

Certainly, one could form such a perception on the basis of almost a crescendo of negative incrementalism which sapped the strength of the Community, beginning with the breakup of

156

the University of East Africa in 1970 as individual bits of Community cooperation were replaced by national institutions.

As expressed in East Africa, however, the incrementalism which so sapped the rejuvenative capability of the Community was presented more generally as "changing times." What was happening to the Community was perhaps less a cause than a reflection of the broader changes in the East African total environment. Lower level Community officials as well as the person in the street often articulated the perception that the Community had "been overwhelmed" or "it wasn't strong enough." This being overridden by events certainly was a prominent feature of the political landscape and one which, although it defied exact temporal or social pinpointing, nevertheless was experienced by many.

How to calculate, for example, the ultimate influence of General Amin's coup in 1971? Many individuals in Kenya saw this as an important blockage to the kind of presidential summit which might have solved at least some of the fundamental problems of the Community. While, on balance, more Tanzanian intellectuals and political types probably held a more ideological or exogenous intrusion-perceptional pattern, a number expressed the view that Amin's continuance as head of Uganda made it impossible for the two states to get together and present a united front to Kenya in order to reduce the existing benefit ratios which they felt favored that country.

Or, how to measure the impact of the Rhodesian UDI in 1965 which set in motion a vast set of reactions which are still being felt today. Zambia, instead of continuing the pattern of transaction flows to the south - where it infrastructurally and economically belonged - turned east and west and thus, through the TanZam railroad drew Tanzania's economic attention southward.

Internal changes in the countries involved also added their down drag to the Community's prospects. The frustrations of implementing the Ujamaa program in Tanzania obviously caused some members of that government to look for scapegoats elsewhere and Kenya became a likely target. While this process was often rationalized in ideological terms, at least part of its genesis had to do with Kenya's economic advances in relation to Tanzania's accomplishments in the same area.

The "times changed" viewpoint was also evident in the post-mortems of some Community officials. The Community, they argued, had played an important role after independence, now events had run away from its control, its structure was too weak in the face of these changed realities, even though some of the concomitant expectations remained. So, they argued, the Community would die over time, new international structures would be created and the phoenix factor will result in a better fit between institution and existing realities. This almost organic image was also put forth by a number of OAU officials who saw in the demise of the EAC an opportunity to greatly broaden the base for regional development in East Africa by including Zambia, Botswana, Malawi, Rwanda and Burundi, even Ethiopia and Somalia.

Perceptional Pattern #6:   Sub-National Politics Proved Too Powerful

Although one could argue that the broadest perceptional pattern would group all political phenomena under one heading, or that the rubric "changing times" could adequately house sub-national political developments as well as the international ones cited above, there is yet another perceptional pattern which is at once more than and less than these.

While it is true that the original Community treaty gave too much power to the presidents of the three states and that in this context the failure of Kenyatta, Nyerere and Amin to rectify the situation contains enough validity to be acceptable, some have argued that it was political fighting and one-upmanship within the governments of Kenya and Tanzania which ultimately did in the Community. Some actors saw the problem and turmoil and lack of presidential interest an opportunity to enhance their political and economic as well as bureaucratic positions.

We shall be returning to the bureaucratic dimension in due course, but it should be pointed out in this context, that several prominent scholars identified this pattern as

158

far back as the failure to form the East African Federation. Thomas Frank, for example, described that failure as "... a near-classic example of political wreaking,"(23) And Donald Rothchild prophetically declared:

> Since the crucial actors on the political scene tend to be alike in the manner in which they chafe at institutional or interest group restraints as well as in their conception of politics as something approximately a 'zero-sum' game, little flexibility is left for such essential requisites of federation as compromise and tolerance.(24)

Just as the attempt to form the East African Federation eventually foundered on the rocks of sub-national politics (individual, group and bureaucratic), so too, at some point to certain political actors the Community became more valuable dead than alive. Stated quite simply, international contraction meant bureaucratic expansion for those ministries which took over responsibility for Community services and assets. In other words, one way to view the outcome of the situation is to see pro-Community individuals losing power to bureaucratic actors who had reason to gain from its demise.(25) For localized (albeit valuable) gains, various bureaucratic actors push for a national policy which will benefit them in terms organizational "health" and power.(26)

Although they were often reluctant to state such views in these bald terms, some Kenyan officials held similar perceptions, as did Community officials at the highest levels (unless they had been absorbed into the appropriate bureaucracy, in which case they tended to espouse a different belief-set for the breakup). Certainly, whether at the bureaucratic or the national level (and indeed even within the ideological realm) the assumption that for actor A (ministry or country) to "win," actor B (ministry or Community agency or country) had to "lose" altered the very context of and basis for the Community in the first place. The concept on which the community was based was on what in game theory is termed a "minimax" strategy; that is, one actor may receive more in the way of a payoff than another actor, but even the losing actor will be better off than he would have been if he had not played at all.

In the waning months, if not years, of its existence, the Community certainly was viewed by more and more partici- pants as a zero-sum situation, and however often independent observers would point to the advantages of returning to a minimum-maximum, or positive sum, view of the situation, the perceptional alternations could not be reserved.

These six perceptional patterns are not, of course, en- tirely mutually exclusive. Individual actors and observers could espouse more than one or hold portions of several. But, in any event, I have tried to underscore the notion that whatever ultimately caused the downfall of the East African Community, the perceptions concerning that downfall will probably remain as important as the reasons themselves in determining what efforts, if any, develop to reconstitute the Community and in what directions that reconstruction will go.

For what it is worth, my own perceptions concerning the validity of the six perceptional patterns are as follows. While there were real elements of all six patterns involved in the breakup, I believe that several impacted more impor- tantly on the eventual breakup than others. The differing ideological backgrounds and assumptions of three member states, for example, had less of an ultimate impact than the failure of the political leadership of those states to solve the problems which they faced-before those problems took on the appearance of being insoluble.

The fact that the major decisions concerning the Com- munity could only be made at the highest levels of the re- spective governments was a key structural flaw in the Com- munity arrangement which was exacerbated by the processes of subnational politics within those governments. When it be- came clear that international contraction would mean bureau- cratic expansions for some key ministries and the Community was therefore more valuable dead than alive, the momentum for disintegration became extremely powerful if not irrestible.

Thus the central political aspects at the core of the disintegration process loom larger in the final analysis than say the elements of exogenous intrusion or the changing nature of the times. There was, in my judgment, no _a priori_ reason why the Community could not deal with the changes of the 1970's had the political leadership the will to maintain it.

At the same time, those who cited the "economic realities" are not incorrect in stressing that these forces made
the political leadership less likely to opt for continued
integration rather than disintegration. It will therefore be
very interesting to see if the recent overthrow of General
Amin and the manner of that overthrow (which obviously re-
engaged Julius Nyerere deeply into East African affairs) will
have anything like a salutary impact on future moves toward
integration in the area.

Chapter VII

Footnotes

1. See, for example, Agrippah T. Mugomba, "Regional Organizations and Africa Underdevelopment: The Collapse of the East African Community," The Journal of Modern African Studies, Vol. XVI, No. 2 (1978), pp. 261-272, and Richard Fredland, "Who Killed the East African Community?", paper prepared for delivery at the International Studies Association meeting, March, 1979.

2. An earlier draft of this paper was presented at the International Studies Association meeting in Toronto, March, 1979, and I am most grateful for the many helpful and incisive comments of Arthur Hazlewood, Richard Fredland, John Ravenhill and Domenico Mazzeo. It subsequently appeared in World Affairs, Vol. 142, No. 1 (Summer, 1979), pp. 45-56.

3. Donald Rothchild (ed.), Politics of Integration: An East African Documentary (Nairobi: East African Publishing House, 1968), P. Dormi Delupis, East African Community and Common Market (London: William Cloves and Sons, 1970), T. M. Frank et al., Why Federations Fail (New York: New York University Press, 1968), A. Hazlewood, Economic Integration: The East African Experience (New York: St. Martin's Press, 1975), A. J. Hughes, East Africa: The Search For Unity (Baltimore: Penguin Books, 1963), Joseph Nye, Pan Africanism and East African Integration (Cambridge: Harvard University Press, 1965), Kenneth Ingham, A History of East Africa (New York: Praeger, 1965) and Walter Elkan and Leslie Nulty "Economic Links in East Africa," in D. A. Low and Alison Smith (eds.), History of East Africa (Oxford: Clarendon Press, 1976).

4. Roberta Wohlstetter, Pearl Harbor: Warning and Decision (Stanford: Hoover Institute, 1962), p. 302.

5. In this regard, I am most grateful to Dean Alfred H. Fuchs and the Bowdoin Mellon Fellowship Committee for their support and for a Fulbright-Hays Grant, which enabled me to do field work in East Africa during 1977

and 1978.

6. Robert Jervis, "Hypotheses on Misperceptions," World Politics, Vol. XX, No. 3 (April, 1968), p. 460.

7. Graham Allison, Essence of Decision (Boston: Little Brown, 1971).

8. Anthony Hughes also argues that different view of infra-structural usage greatly contributed to the decline in all three governments' notion of reciprocal benefits. See his "Community of Disinterest," Africa Report (March/April, 1975), pp. 37-43.

9. For an insightful study of the TanZam project, see K. S. Mutukwa, Politics of the Tanzania-Zambia Railproject: A Study of Tanzania-China-Zambia Relations (Washington: University Press of America, 1977).

10. Tanzania's ideological expectations and their lack of fulfillment under the existing Community setup are clearly seen in the Demas Commission Report.

11. Tim Shaw, for example, probably goes too far in labeling what transpired as Kenyan "sub-imperialism," at least with regard to the ideological connotations of that word: Timothy Shaw, "International Stratification in Africa: Sub-Imperialism in Southern and Eastern Africa." Journal of Southern Africa, Vol. II, No. 2 (April, 1977), pp. 145-165.

12. This not only involved surviving fake "plots" to justify massacres of both civilians and military personnel, but real ones as well, and making sure that however shattered the Ugandan economy, there were enough tangible rewards to keep the key elements of the military loyal to him.

13. Jervis, "Misperceptions," p. 472.

14. Africa Confidential, Vol. XVIII, No. 13, June 24, 1977.

15. The Community also suffered from this situation. When the East African Post and Telecommunication headquarters

was to be moved to Kampala, many of its employees refused to go, fearing to even put themselves in Uganda
no matter what their status.

16. For example, expatriate employees engaged by the Community to pilot the ferry boats on Lake Victoria objected
to being "harrassed" by TANU stalwarts about their
failure to maintain adequate garden plots.

17. David Baldwin, "Foreign Aid, Intervention, and Influence," World Politics (April, 1969), pp. 425-447.

18. Carried to its macro-level, of course, this argument
could explain the breakup in purely economic terms. The
Tanzanian government, like any prudent businessman,
could not continue to run a $30 million trade deficit
with Kenya. See Africa Special Report, "Death of a
Community," Africa #72 (August, 1977), p. 44.

19. In 1978, Kenya's 500,000 visitors left behind an estimated $50 million.

20. This argument, of course, cuts both ways. On the one
hand, some companies (such as British Midland Airways)
stood to gain from the breakup (by providing the planes
for the new Kenya Air). Many others did not. For example, the African Airlines Association (AFRAA) deplored the breakup of the Community and "... worked hard
behind the scene to avert the present crisis," Africa
Special Report, "The Final Rupture," Africa #76 (December, 1977), pp. 64-65.

21. Allison's phrase could, of course, apply equally to the
rational actor paradigm, the organizational process
paradigm and the bureaucratic politics paradigm. In
terms of the Community and its officials' perceptions
the choice of the paradigm would not seem to alter the
dominant-inference pattern in any case.

22. Fredland, "Who Killed the East African Community,"
pp. 10-11.

23. Thomas Frank, "East African Federation" in Frank et al.,
Why Federations Fail, p. 3.

24. Donald Rothchild (ed.), <u>Politics of Integration</u>, p. 7.

25. See, for example, Allison, <u>Essence of Decision</u>, pp. 145-184.

26. This, of course, could also be applied to bureaucratic activity within companies as well as ministries. See Peter Blunt, "Social and Organizational Structures in East Africa: A Case For Participation," <u>Journal of Modern African Studies</u>, Vol. XVI, No. 3 (1968), pp. 433-449.

CHAPTER VIII

Plowshares Into Swords: The Former Member
States and the 1978 - 1979 War

Hrach Gregorian

I. Introduction

"You are not ready," is the same argument the
imperialists have always used . . . Is it not
going to be the most curious piece of irony if
we, the African Nationalists, who have always
wanted unity, were to inherit and use this
argument to perpetuate colonial divisions?
                                    Julius Nyerere(1)

History has a way of playing cruel tricks on even the
most prescient of observers, and Julius Nyerere can be for-
given for not having foreseen in 1960 the events which were
to transpire in East Africa almost twenty years later.
Nyerere was certainly not alone in embracing the dream of
federation. His neighbors in the region expressed a similar
commitment to "Pan-Africanism." Little did they know then
that as independent Africa came of age, not only these hopes,
but more modest ones for economic integration, would be
dashed on the rocks of Realpolitik more commonly associated
with the older colonial powers.

The Chapter which follows focuses on East Africa's
brush with the most baneful of the "imperial" world's numerous untidy experiences. It is an examination of the six-
month war waged by Uganda and Tanzania in 1978-1979. More
precisely, it is an attempt to address a number of questions
both on a case specific basis and in the context of a larger
concern with factors contributing to disintegration among
regional groupings in the developing world.

Broadly stated, we wish to ascertain why the war broke
out; how it was waged; what its immediate repercussions were;
and possible implications of the reversal for the countries
directly involved, for East Africa, and for integrative
schemes in general. These are obviously ambitious goals for
a work of this length, and early date and we make no claim to
exhaustiveness in treatment. Our major objective is to gain
an overview and some insight into what appear to be the most
salient issues.

The study is composed of essentially three interrelated
components. The first endeavors to analyze, on a comparative

basis, the underlying factors within Uganda and Tanzania contributing to the outbreak of hostilities. The second undertakes to explain the actual conduct of the war from a military, strategic and political standpoint. The third, and concluding segment, attempts to determine what linkage, if any, existed between the East African Community experience and the 1978-1979 crisis and the short-term impact for East Africa, as well as more general lessons, of the war.

II. The Guns of October

If formation of the East African Community (EAC) was "not the product of a sudden burst of political inspiration in 1967,"[2] the spectacle of a full-scale conflict between former members Uganda and Tanzania just over a decade later was in fact the consequence of a rather precipitous decline in member state relations following the overthrow of Uganda's Milton Obote by General Idi Amin in 1971. The relatively successful record of the Community prior to this event underscores its importance as a watershed in the ten-year history of the EAC.[3]

Amin's sanguinary putsch had raised the ire of Tanzania's President Julius Nyerere who not only refused to recognize the so-called "illegal regime" in Uganda, but also provided asylum for Obote, a close friend. Nyerere's opposition remained steadfast throughout Amin's seven-year reign of terror, while his harboring of Obote served as a source of constant irritation for the General who feared the deposed President's close proximity and silently insidious activities.

Amin's worst fears were confirmed once, in 1972, when Ugandan exiles loyal to Obote launched an ill-fated attack on their homeland using northern Tanzania as a staging area. On that occasion, it took the timely efforts of the Organization of African Unity and Somali President Muhammad Siyad Barre to prevent an escalation and expansion of the conflict. A settlement was eventually reached in Mogadishu wherein both sides pledged their commitment to the prevention of a similar incident and to the establishment of a demilitarized zone. Left undecided still was the fate of Milton Obote -- a circumstance which continued to poison relations between Kampala and Dar es Salaam. Thereafter, Amin took to periodically claiming that his country was being invaded by Tanzania; charges which were openly scoffed at by Nyerere, who along with other observers viewed them, for the most part, as mere ploys intended to distract attention from Uganda's steadily worsening internal situation.

Thus it was that little heed was paid to a Ugandan radio broadcast, on October 12, 1978, which once again sounded the familiar invasion alarm. Following past practice, a military spokesman (usually Amin), announced that "a battalion of Tanzanian troops crossed into Uganda on the west side of Lake Victoria . . . [October 11] and advanced 8 miles burning houses, destroying life and property of people and seriously wounding three Ugandan soldiers."(4) Tanzania's response was to label the charge "nonsense": an assessment which appeared accurate in light of statements made by a police official in the town of Mbarara, pinpointed by the Ugandans as the area around which fighting purportedly took place, and by Ugandan refugees in Nairobi who had taken part in the aborted 1972 invasion. The police official said all was calm in his town and he knew of no fighting, while emigre sources reported having no information regarding a move against Amin. The consensus also among diplomats in the area was that there was scant likelihood of an actual military invasion taking place.(5)

What had, in fact, occurred, became clear sometime later when a tangled web, intimately linked with Uganda's domestic woes, finally unraveled.

Explaining Amin's Motives

Throughout Amin's tenure, his major source of strength, and towards the end, his only source was the military. As the Ugandan economy crumbled, with crippling inflation and black market activities running rampant (according to some sources, of the 12,600 tons of Arabic coffee produced in 1977, only 2,500 tons had been exported, the rest having been smuggled out.(6) Coffee accounts for roughly 90% of Uganda's exports). Amin began to rely more heavily on the army to suppress growing acts of rebellion. But the army's continued "loyalty" depended on delivery of high-priced military hardware and the bestowal of special privileges. With

170

Western aid cut off, Arab monies trickling, rather than pouring, in, exports to the West went down dramatically,(7) and the price of coffee plummeting from $8,000 a ton in 1977 to $2,000 a ton just a year later, Amin could scarce afford the cost of continued support.(8) An ambitious three-year development plan unveiled in 1976 had not only failed to resolve his cash flow problems, but had further exacerbated relations with the armed forces by placing, for the first time, economic growth ahead of military expansion (9)

Rumblings throughout the soldiery soon followed, precipitating outbreaks of mutiny and other signs of disenchantment. To stave off any further erosion of authority, Amin did what he knew best. He massacred thousands of soliders suspected of lese-majeste, placed several ministers under house arrest, sacked leaders of army regiments, and ousted vice-president Mustapha Adrisi (later involved in a serious automobile accident construed by his supporters to have been a near-successful assassination attempt).(10) A rift developed between the Muslim ruling hierarchy, setting Amin and his small Kakwa tribe against the Madi-Lugbara tribes to which Adrisi, among other discharged leaders, belonged. An eleventh fruitless attempt on Amin's life was followed by still further unrest in the armed forces.

The October 11 disturbance was symptomatic of the problem now surfacing with increasing frequency throughout the Ugandan countryside. A rebellion had apparently taken place at the Malire barracks, in Mbarara, situated approximately 31 miles from the Tanzanian border. There, about 150 troops loyal to Amin had been killed by members of the Simba regiment believed to support former vice-president General Adrisi. The mutineers had fled, perhaps with some Tanzanian cooperation, across the border, followed by Amin and his forces. Once on foreign soil, Amin trumped up charges of a Tanzanian invasion to justify and expand his own punitive strike.(11)

The general evidently had several motives for instigating a border war. It was a convenient cover up for the incident at the Malire barracks as well as an inveterate tactic for uniting the people (especially the army), against an apparent common enemy. The occasion could also be utilized to extirpate Ugandan exiles in the region, long a thorn in

Amin's side, and provide his restive soliders with some welcome booty. A final withdrawal would then be made contin-
gent upon Tanzanian guarantees to permanently trammel anti-
Amin forces on its territory.

III. The War Expands

If Amin's initial cries of invasion were taken lightly,
a Tanzanian communique, on October 31, announcing that its
armed forces were engaged in battle with invading Ugandan
troops "at a place in the West Lake [Victoria] region," was
not. According to Tanzanian reports, the Ugandans had begun
their invasion on Monday, October 30, after undertaking week-
end air strikes into northern Tanzania.(12) The Tanzanians,
taken unawares and ill-prepared, provided little resistance
to Amin's well-orchestrated dragonnade.

By mid-week, to to three thousand Ugandan soliders,
backed by tanks and heavy artillery, had overrun the remote
Kagera salient in northwestern Tanzania and annexed 710-
square-miles of largely uninhabited swampland. On Wednesday,
November 1, Radio Uganda, officially acknowledging Amin's
"conquest," declared the establishment of a new boundary at
the Kagera River about 20 miles south of the original border (see map). In the broadcast, a military spokesman (read
Amin), boasted: "All Tanzanians in the area must know that
they are now under direct rule of the Conqueror of the British Empire, Field Marshal Amin." Referring to the "super-
sonic speed" with which the annexation was accomplished,
Amin also used the occasion to accuse Tanzanian soldiers of
"cowardice" adding that they were unable to "face the challenge of Ugandan troops."(13)

Such chest beating was not to serve the Field Marshal
well. A humiliated Nyerere vowed to hit back hard at the
"barbarian" and urged his forces to drive "this snake from
our house."(14) It would appear that a decision was made
early on in Dar to make the rude Amin's last hurrah and thus
not only to repulse the invading army, but to destroy the
very government under which it served. Besides personal
animosity(15) and initial embarrassment, Nyerere had other
motives for ousting Amin. In the months preceeding the Ugandan invasion, Amin had become involved in the Zimbabwe Rho-

desian War by providing training bases for moderate black
nationalists. These very same groups had agreed to a compromise settlement with the white dominated government of
Prime Minister Ian D. Smith. Such action highly antagonized
countries like Mozambique and Angola which were allied with
Tanzania in supporting Smith's nemesis, the more radical
Patriotic Front.

SOURCE: Dave Cook,
The Washington Post

By removing Amin, Nerere would at once secure his
northern border; perhaps install an ally with a compatible
socialist system, thereby strengthening Tanzania's bargaining
position vis-a-vis Kenya; and gain the necessary latitude to
effectively deal with his consuming interest, southern
Africa.(16) The war could also serve to draw attention away
from Tanzania's own domestic woes which included badly deteriorating roadways, cancelled flights, inefficiences at its
one port, and chronic shortages of such basic staples as
butter and cooking oil.(17)

Crossing the Rubicon

Overcoming a number of start-up problems, not least of

173

which were the logistics of mounting a counter-offensive 700 miles northwest of Dar es Salaam and mastering the use of sophisticated weaponry in an actual combat situation (one of Tanzania's first acts was to shoot down three of its own Soviet-supplied MiGs),(18) Nyerere's forces began to push back the invaders in early November. The scale of fighting was relatively modest due to the limited arsenal possessed by both sides and the inaccessible terrain. Early Ugandan demolition of the Taka bridge, which spanned the 60-foot-wide Kagera River and served as the only major link between the occupied territory and the rest of Tanzania, rendered initial Tanzanian sorties rather ineffectual.

The Ugandans, some 2,000 to 3,000 strong, remained dug in on the north bank of the river using Soviet-supplied T-54 tanks and artillery to easily fend off small arms and mortar fire from the other side. But with the introduction of additional reinforcements and more accurate heavy bombardment, the Tanzanians were eventually able to establish a bridgehead on the contested area. From there, they soon began to expand the war into the Ugandan heartland.

International Reaction

The intensification of fighting was matched by a growing flurry of diplomatic activity both within the continent and abroad. The U.S. State Department issued a statement supporting "fully and completely" Tanzania's demand for a Ugandan withdrawal, while the Soviet Union, apparently embarrassed by Amin's antics, quietly removed its technicians and advisors from the country shortly after the outbreak of hostilities.(19) Mediation efforts by African nations began with a Libyan offer, on November 5, to act as go-between in whatever actions the two sides chose to undertake to resolve the conflict. Although acceptable to Uganda, the offer was spurned by Nyerere who was not unmindful of the close relationship enjoyed by Tripoli and Kampala.

November 5 also saw Kenya's President, Daniel Arap Moi, releasing an ambiguously worded pronouncement calling on Uganda to withdraw its troops "if" it had violated Tanzanian sovereignty.(20) Such a gesture did not sit well with Nyerere, nor did the stance taken by the Organization of African Unity (OAU). The cardinal principle of the OAU charter is acceptance of existing national boundaries, but try as he may, Nyerere could not get the Organization to formally condemn Amin's flagrant violation.(21) His most infuriating experience, however, may well have been with a small group of African leaders, including Sudanese President (and OAU head), Gafaar Nimeiry and Nigerian leader Olusegun Obasanjo, all of whom, according to Nyerere, asked him to forswear the use of force and undertake peaceful negotiations. "What was there to negotiate," Nyerere would later ask, "our own territory?"(22) What remaining doubts he may have had about moving unilaterally to punish and contain Amin were evidently erased thereafter.

Amin Evacuates

Under heavy pressure from the OAU and, perhaps, in response to the serious preparations for war inside Tanzania, Idi Amin declared, on November 8, that Uganda was prepared to fully withdraw its forces from northern Tanzania as soon as assurances were given that Tanzania would "never invade Uganda again" and that it would stop arming Ugandan exiles.(23) One week later, whether driven out forcibly, as Tanzania claimed, or moving on their own initiative, as was the claim in Uganda, Amin's forces were back inside the country's internationally recognized borders. "We have done what we were asked [by the OAU]," one high ranking Ugandan official remarked upon this occasion, "what more can anyone want?"(24) The answer was not long in coming.

Nyerere Advances

On November 26 The Sunday News in Tanzania carried an editorial asserting that Tanzania would not interfere in the internal affairs of its neighbor. The editorial read in part: "We must guard against our nationalism being turned into chauvinism, promoting the violation of principles which we are fighting to uphold."(25) Less than 24 hours later, Tanzanian troops crossed the border into Uganda, advancing toward the strategically important town of Masaka, on the main route to Kampala. The border war had now reached a third and fateful phase, one which was to last some four and a half months, ending with the capture of Kampala and the final ouster of Amin.

IV. Politico-Military Factors

On paper, the Ugandan-Tanzanian War pitted two fairly evenly matched military forces against one another.(26) Both sides enjoyed rough parity with regard to the range of guns in their possession, although there was little in the Ugandan arsenal to match Tanzania's Soviet-supplied BM 21 multiple rocket-launchers (20 km range) and 130 mm long-range guns. Uganda's 15 Russian made T54 and T55 tanks were broadly equivalent to the over 30 Chinese-supplied T59 and T62 tanks owned by the Tanzanians, while the MiG-21s flown by the two air forces were also roughly equivalent. (If the Ugandan-Tanzanian War demonstrated anything militarily, however, it was the very limited utility of both tanks and air support in the type of ground combat engaged in. In the end, it was radar-controlled artillery and rocket fire which proved to be Tanzania's chief asset.) The 20,000 man Ugandan army faced some 25,000 troops on the Tanzanian side each equipped with similar Russian manufactured 76 and 122 mm field guns and mobile surface-to-air missles.

As is often the case, however, such quantitative figures tell nothing of the deeper socio-political and psychological factors which spelled the difference once the fighting commenced. Under fire, Amin's vaunted military machine turned out to be a paper tiger which had, for reasons discussed presently, neither the will nor the capacity to fight even a defensive war in its own backyard against an attacking force facing enormous logistical problems and relatively unfamiliar terrain.

Amin, in fact, may have lost this war long before the firing ceased on the battlefield. His army, having been plagued by purges and factional rivalries, was woefully inadequate. (One Western diplomat, brushing aside suggestions that material shortages might have accounted for Uganda's dismal performance, commented: "Amin's problem isn't lack of hardware, his problem is that his army is no damn good.")(27) The officer corps, depleted of all its British-trained members, was divided between pro-Adrisi and pro-Amin groups more interested in settling old scores than working to save the regime -- the confusion touched off by the Tanzanian advance facilitated, it seems, the squaring of more than one account.(28)

The rest of the armed forces proved either incompetent (after Tanzania shot down 6 of Amin's MiG fighters, his air force withered to only four pilots trained to fly such aircraft, two of whom Amin did not trust), or disloyal; in one of many similar acts of sabotage, Ugandan soldiers from Mubende dispatched to the Tanzania border wrecked their vehicles and armoured tanks along the road and then reported back their inability to move further. Amin never mobilized the entire army for fear they might turn against him, and he kept many soldiers unarmed even as he ordered them into battle.(29) Those troops still loyal to the regime (mostly Nubians, often mercenaries), experienced a steady fall in morale as supplies of ammunition, food, and transport vehicles quickly gave out.

The General's ineffectual leadership style further aggravated Uganda's difficulties. Amin evidently failed to take Nyerere's challenge very seriously, particularly during the early stage of the war, and remained confused as to Nyerere's intent throughout much of the subsequent months of fighting. He had also undertaken little contingency planning and, therefore, could set to work no concrete policy to repel the invading forces once the war expanded. As one well-placed source in Kampala saw it: "The President is helpless. His comprehension of what is happening in the country is at best blurred and, strangely for a commander of the armed forces, he appears not to have any coherent strategy to deal with the situation."(30)

It might be stated in defense of Amin or, more accurately, as a final indictment, that he was in effect waging war on four fronts simultaneously. First, of course, he had the invading Tanzanian forces to contend with composed of well-trained regular supported by increasingly accurate artillery and rocket fire. Then there was his own army; underpaid, demoralized, mutinous, harboring pro-Obote elements, divided by ethnic and other differences, retreating in disarray after occasional skirmishes, refusing to fight, or worse, joining hands with the enemy at the first opportunity. A third and most effective front was provided by Ugandan exiles and rebel forces operating within and outside the country to raise money, speak out publicly against the regime, and engage in guerrilla activities.(31) Finally, the domestic population, having long suffered under Amin and his troops, provided little support for the war effort. They chose, rather, either to aid the guerrillas directly, or undertake other more general acts of civil insurrection.

In the face of all this, there was little more Amin could do than ride in his jeep from one disastrous battle scene to another reassuring the growing list of skeptics that he was still in control of Uganda. When all seemed lost, he made a desperate plea for help to what remaining friends he had in the Moslem world. Only the Libyans were able to respond with more than a token gesture, pouring in some 2,000 men and supportive material.(32) For their troubles Qaddafi's poorly trained young soldiers received a quick dose of Tanzanian and rebel fire power, sustaining 600 wounded or dead in their first weeks of battle. In fact, according to the Moroccan News Agency, the Libyan government was reduced in the end to paying Amin's enemies twenty million dollars to secure the safe evacuation of its hard-pressed expeditionary forces.(33)

V. Julius Would Not Be Caesar

A remaining question in light of the preceding discussion is why, with Amin's countless difficulties, it took the Tanzanians over four months to overrun Uganda. There were, unquestionably, logistical problems resulting from the rough terrain and the long distance separating Dar and Kampala. The attackers also moved slowly and cautiously to incur as little loss a possible. And the Libyans, no doubt, helped Amin win a short reprieve in March.

But the major factor contributing to the long duration of the war was Nyerere's wish to portray the affair ostensibly as an internal struggle amongst the Ugandans with Tanzania aiding the anti-Amin side only in a supporting capacity. Doing otherwise would have entailed openly flouting the very dictates of the OAU charter for which Amin had been so roundly criticized initially. Nyerere, "Africa's conscience," was loathe to risk similar disapprobation, both internationally, and from Tanzania's own small but influential intellectual elite. (Thus it was that the government-controlled press in Dar assiduously underscored the purported internecine nature of the war while consistently downplaying

178

the crucial role played by Tanzanian soldiers.)

Nyerere took a number of steps to "Ugandanize" the 1978-1979 War. In late December, 1978, he brought together in Nairobi Ugandan exiles of various ideologies and tribal affinities -- many of whom had undergone military training in several East African countries -- to form a united front against Amin. He appealed to the assemblage to join in the war effort, adding that he did not wish to have his troops regarded as an occupying force if Amin were toppled.(34) Furthermore, he promised that no leader would be forced upon the Ugandan people once the country had been liberated. This last assurance was critical to certain tribal elements like the Bugandans who were not particularly eager to see Nyerere's friend, Obote, return to power for they harbored bitter memories of the autocratic President's treatment of tribes resisting his attempts at national unity. The December meeting adjourned with a general agreement to attempt to consolidate rebel efforts against Amin.

As the best-known Ugandan (and still, the country's only legal President), Obote was a key component in Nyerere's scheme who could not be kept silent for long. He was brought out in January; significantly, to reject Amin's allegations that Tanzania was aiming to restore him to power, and to call on his countrymen to rise up against "the fascist dictator" who had turned Uganda into "a human slaughterhouse."(35) The well-rehearsed Obote was at pains to add that the situation in Uganda was in the people's hands and that only they, not foreign troops, could liberate the country.(36)

A concerted effort was undertaken, thereafter, to co-ordinate the activities of the exile forces (whose ranks were steadily being swelled by deserters from Amin's army), and guerrilla organizations, like the Save Uganda Movement (SUM) and the Front for National Salvation (FRONSA), operating within Uganda. To allow the insurgents time to mobilize and eventually mount what would hopefully be a full-scale insurrection, Nyerere held his military advance in check; even though there was little resistance being met on the battlefield. The strategy was to move hard enough to put maximum pressure on Amin yet slow enough to reserve for the Ugandans the largest possible role in the conduct of military and political operations.(37)

Nyerere's plans became particularly apparent in late February and early March when upon securing full control of the southern third of Uganda, he sat and waited for a general uprising throughout the rest of the country. Meanwhile, to be sure that there would be no talk of a possible concilia- tion with Amin, the Tanzanians set peace terms which they knew neither the OAU nor Amin could accept.(38)

The spontaneous insurrection never came. Rebel forces proved to lack the necessary organization (often competing with one another), or the military know-how to go it alone. In reaction, Nyerere stepped up construction of rebel train- ing camps in southern Uganda. At the same time, to achieve a semblance of unity among exile factions, and to create at least a nominal political infrastructure to challenge Amin's (and, presumably, stand ready to assume the reigns of power upon his departure), he helped organize a meeting in Moshi (Tanzania) in late March. At that time, some 100 delegates, representing 18 different factions, voted to form an Ugandan National Liberation Front (UNLF) with an eleven-member Exe- cutive Council headed by Yusufu K. Lule, a moderate, 67-year- old academician.(39) A statement of the UNLF's principles and general policy goals was drafted and released upon this occasion.

The UNLF helped, perhaps, to accelerate Amin's decline. And the rebel forces continued to play a more visible role in the latter stages of fighting. But when Kampala did finally fall, on April 11, it fell primarily to Tanzanian soldiers. The local citizenry, rather than singing songs of praise to the UNLF or Yusufu Lule, greeted the conquerors with chants of "up with Nyerere, down with Amin."(40) Al- though the exiles, as planned, announced the formation of a provisional government, with Lule as President, it was the Tanzanian army which moved through Uganda consolidating military control -- control which, as of this writing, re- mains steadfast.

VI. Conclusion

The Ugandan-Tanzanian War represents the first case in the history of independent Africa where one national success- fully invaded another for the express purpose of unseating the latter's head of state. More striking is the fact that the belligerents, along with Kenya were former members of an economic community which was looked upon by some not only as a model for regional cooperation amongst developing nations, but also, as a precursor to the more ambitious goal of eventual political federation in East Africa. The three neighbors, after all, formed the ideal grouping for just such an integrative scheme; sharing, as they did, similar colonial histories and patterns of white settlement, common tongues in English and Ki-Swahili, interlocking systems of commerce and transportation, and border tribes with overlapping relations and affinities.

And yet, the East African Community failed. It failed the lofty political aspirations of some of its founders and it failed the less exaggerated economic expectations of most of its supporters. More to the point, one year after its demise, ex-partners Uganda and Tanzania were at each other's throats.

The EAC Legacy

The collapse of the East African Community undoubtedly aggravated the already strained relations between Uganda and Tanzania. There was little uncovered in our study, however, directly linking this event with the ensuing military engagement. We conclude, in fact, that Amin and Nyerere would have resorted to war in 1978 even if the EAC had remained intact; much as they almost did in 1973, when a host of extra-community actors intervened to prevent a similar outcome.

War came to East Africa because Uganda was falling apart internally under Amin's misrule. It came because Obote's presence in Tanzania haunted the Field Marshal and further poisoned relations between Dar and Kampala. And it came because Nyerere could neither stomach Amin personally nor accept his presence politically -- facts he made known in no uncertain terms. Furthermore, the absence of a political arm empowered to at least address the issue of conflict resolution would have rendered the EAC virtually inconsequential in any peacemaking efforts once hostilities had commenced (again, as was the case in 1972).

But if the Community's collapse did not provide the immediate spark for the subsequent conflagration, its uneven history and legacy did intensify the bitterness of feeling on all sides and may well have helped to extend the duration of the wdar. For the fact remains that just as economic cooperation may lead to political understanding, so too, under the integrative umbrella of a regional organization, it can contribute to heightened dissidence by effectively forcing separating partners to deal with one another more intimately and for a longer period than it would otherwise be desirable or prudent to.

That Nyerere felt a special animus for Amin is unquestioned. It was the EAC, however, which provided him with the necessary instrumentality to express these sentiments more directly than any public forum could have. Blocking Amin's appointments and refusing to convene the East African Authority with the General in power was not tantamount to an invasion or a formal declaration of war, but it was an effective device for humiliating Amin and making his life more difficult. On the other hand, Amin could strike back by butchering Tanzanian nationals working in Uganda for Community corpirations (which he did). The end result was still further rupture in political relations between Dar and Kampala.

Kenya's experience with the EAC added yet another dimension to the war. Had the new government of President Daniel arap Moi been so inclined, it could have quickly brought Amin to his knees. With passage of the U.S. trade embargo in August, and with reserves of oil and other essential commodities already dangerously low, Uganda had become ever more dependent on Kenya for supplies to carry on the war effort. Moi, however, rejected Tanzania's importunes to cut off Uganda's overland oil supplies and assumed a "neutral" stance.

He did so partially because it was his still untested government's first foreign policy crisis and because his armed forces were outnumbered 2 to 1 by Amin's (although this ratio became irrelevant soon after war broke out). In addition, Kenya was admittedly doing a banner business supplying Uganda with many of the goods she could no longer produce. (Amin had become an even more important customer in

1977, upon Nyerere's closing of the Tanzanian-Kenyan border.) But Moi's key motive for adopting the policy that he did was not so much to prop up Amin, as some Ugandan exiles charged, but to avoid the possible return of Obote -- and, in particular, an Obote so enormously indebted to Nyerere.

The Kenyans did not exactly look with sanguinity upon such a prospect, recalling capitalist-minded President Kenyatta's persistent difficulties with the Nyerere-Obote alliance when the three constituted the leadership of the EAC. Nairobi, having continued with a western-style economic system to out-distance her East African neighbor, was understandably wary -- for geo political as well as economic reasons -- of once again being flanked by two potentially stifling socialist states. In any case, the residue of past bitterness, particularly during the waning days of the EAC, did not leave the Kenyans well disposed to Dar's requests for assistance to topple Amin.

* * *

It is reputed that Francis I, when asked what differences accounted for the constant wars between him and his brother-in-law Charles V, replied: "None whatever. We agree perfectly. We both want Italy."(41) So too, it can be said of the EAC experience that rather than contributing to misunderstanding between Uganda, Tanzania and Kenya, it served to deepen their appreciation for one another's position. Such understanding, unfortunately, rendered war between Nyerere and Amin all but inevitable and forced Moi to assume a "neutral" stance that was distinctly partisan in effect.

Short-Term Impact of War

Uganda.   The Ugandan-Tanzanian War left the already impoverished Ugandan economy in a state of utter exhaustion. Domestic security dissolved to the point where only the presence of the Tanzanian army prevented a complete breakdown of domestic order.   Political battles, growing out of tribal, regional and ideological differences, became the order of the day.   On June 20, 1979, President Lule, just two months in office, was removed by the National Consultative Council -- the ruling arm of the UNLF. Lule's replacement by Godfrey Binaisa, a former attorney general under Obote who had been forced out in 1967 as a result of differences with the former President over the Ugandan Constitution, unleashed still further unrest.

Although a member of the dominant Baganda tribe, Binaisa was no favorite among fellow tribesmen who accused him of treason in having originally joined Obote's government; a government which had deposed the traditional king of the Baganda, the Kabaka. Demonstrations and strikes against Binaisa reflected, among other sentiments, fear in some quarters that despite past differences, the new President was, in effect, serving as a stalking horse for Obote, now ready to return to power. Their fears, it appears, were only partially warranted. For it was not to be Binaisa, but rather his Labor Minister, Paulo Muwanga (Muwanga also served as the chairman of the six-member military commission of the UNLF), who would serve as Obote's stalking horse. Muwanga, a long-time ally of Obote, overthrew Binaisa in May (1980) and began military rule with the avowed intention to hold elections in September. Before the end of May, Obote was back in Uganda pledging to work for "national reconstruction and reconciliation," and promising to run for his former office when elections do take place. Thus the stage was finally set for the reascension of Julius Nyerere's close friend.

Tanzania. Tanzania's burdens far transcended mere criticism from unappreciative Ugandans. Estimates of the total cost for unseating Amin hovered around the $500 million mark. Given Dar's near encounter with bankruptcy even before the outbreak of hostilities (she suffered a $280 million balance of payments deficit in 1978),(42) the immediate effect of the war was to place Tanzania's economy in a more precarious state than at virtually any other period since independence. Postponement of development projects, shortages in foreign exchange, expansion of already acute transport problems, and a decline in the growth of export crops (both because militia-men had to be taken away from their farms and because they had to be fed once in battle), all have ensued.

Thus the most-aided nation in Africa -- 65% of Tanzania's development budget and 50% of her public sector investments are externally financed -- (43) was once again forced to turn West for additional fiscal assistance. Such assistance, incidentally, has not been fast in coming because of donors' reluctance to shift funds from development to budgetary support, especially when such support is earmarked basically for war relief.

Nyerere's straitened economic circumstances have also undermined Tanzania's role as the leader oof the "front-line states" in the struggle against Zimbabwe Rhodesia. Forced to turn inward, many Tanzanians have come to question the feasibility of simultaneously addressing problems to the South. Remarked one official: ". . . it's a question of balance. We cannot neglect Tanzania's development for the sake of African liberation."(44) Complications have developed to the North as well.

At the July 1979 summit conference of the OAU, both Sudan and Nigeria moved to condemn Nyerere for intervening in Uganda, not withdrawing troops promptly after Amin's defeat, and playing too large a role in postwar Ugandan politics, including the Lule/Binaisa affair. The Sudanese had further cause for complaint. Arab to the north and black African to the south, they feared the revival of North-South tensions as Sudanese mercenaries in the employ of Amin returned home armed. The ranks of these soldiers were swelled by civilians and still other forces loyal to Amin drifting across the border on a regular basis to create additional security problems.

It was no accident that the OAU summit served as a forum for reproving Nyerere. His actions had damaged the organization's overall standing and led some members to conclude that without certain basic changes in the charter, the OAU would now gain a reputation for ineffectiveness in times of crisis similar to that of the United Nations. Consequently, outgoing Chairman Nimeiry of the Sudan and his successor, Liberian President William R. Tolbert, moved to create a five-member body, composed of representative heads of state, who would be empowered in crisis situations to make decisions binding on OAU members. The two also endorsed the idea of a pan-African force to police truces between feuding states.

Kenya. Kenya too, did not escape the war unscathed. Her unwillingness to cut off Amin's supplies not only angered

Tanzania but left her on less than cordial terms with members of the new Ugandan regime, some of whom recalled Nairobi's mistreatment and, in some cases, incarceration of Ugandan exiles before and during the war. For their part, Kenyan security chiefs charged that many Ugandans posing as exiles and anti-Amin guerrillas were often little more than "thugs and dangerous criminals." Whatever the case may have been, the wave of lawlessness sweeping through Uganda at war's end spilled into Kenya causing serious disturbances there. The initial result was the forcible repatriation of more than 3,000 Ugandans by Moi. Kenya's apprehensions about Nyerere's plans for Uganda were aggravated by the May coup and the prospect of Obote's return.

One last point must be made with regard to the precedent set by Tanzania's actions in Uganda. A number of analysts have branded it a dangerous one which may someday return to haunt not only the entire continent, but its titular moral voice as well. We think not.

African leaders are unlikely to engage in similar acts, not so much out of moral compulsion, as out of military and economic disablement. Tanzania, one of the poorest nations on the continent, suffered significant economic hardship in defeating Amin. Had there been a modicum of resistance within Uganda, or more than halfhearted external support, a war of attrition would have ensued leading to an enervating stalemate. Neither regime could escape the domestic fallout which would invariably accompany such an eventuality.

The chaotic war did not end so much with a Tanzanian triumph as it did with a caving in of an isolated dictator who found himself fighting on several fronts simultaneously. What victory Nyerere could claim soon turned pyrrhic as his burdens steadily mounted. The lessons in all this would be, we believe, unmistakable to any potential "king maker" or other adventurer on the continent.

* * *

One highly sympathetic student of regional integration has written:

Scholars studying integration in Africa must

remember the primacy of politics and not be
misled by assumptions natural to "developed"
societies. It is important to pay attention
to social, historical, and economic factors,
but too much time in the archives or statistical libraries will be spent at the cost of
diversion from the main factors -- the political elite and its ideology and interests.(45)

The breakdown of relations in East Africa adds additional emphasis to this noteworthy caveat. It was a political breakdown intimately linked to personal, ideological and
national differences between Nyerere and Amin. Without the
presence of the numerous factors found in groupings of more
advanced industrialized nations, to overcome and otherwise
mute elite sector antipathies and render the system less
vulnerable to sub-systemic fluctuations, it remained only a
question of time before the two sides came to blows and
blighted the hopes of more liberal multilateralists.

It may well be that until the "assumptions natural to
'developed' societies" become equally applicable to the
developing world, the personal and philosophical predilec-
tions of national leaders will continue to play a primary
casual function in regional and/or economic federative
schemes. One would hope, however, in light of how long and
arduous the march toward "modernity" for Europe and other
industrialized powers has been, that some hitherto unknown
intervening variables will mercifully alter the equation
rendering the developing countries' experience less trauma-
tic. Current trends do not augur well.

Chapter VIII

Footnotes

1. Quoted in Joseph S. Nye Jr., <u>Pan-Africanism and East African Integration</u> (Cambridge, Mass.: Harvard University Press, 1967), p. 175.

2. See Allen Springer's "Chronology" earlier in this book.

3. This is not to say, of course, that the Community's demise was due solely to a single cause. As Christian Potholm and Richard Fredland suggest in previous chapters, the break-up resulted from the cumulative effect of a complex set of interrelated factors. The rise of Amin did, nevertheless, mean that "Uganda ceased to be an effective participant in Community decisions and the balance of the Community's tripartite structure disappeared." Arthur Hazlewood, Chapter V.

4. <u>New York Times</u>, October 13, 1978, p. 11.

5. <u>Ibid.</u>, October 14, 1978, p. 32; <u>The Weekly Review</u> (Nairobi), (November 3, 1978), p. 14.

6. <u>To the Point</u> (Transvaal), Vol. IIX, No. 5 (February 2, 1979), p. 39; <u>New Africa</u> (London), No. 37 (January, 1979), p. 14.

7. It was perhaps no mere coincidence that on the day of the alleged Tanzanian invasion (August 11) President Jimmy Carter signed into law a bill severing U.S. trade links with Uganda.

8. <u>Africa</u> (London), No. 92 (April, 1979), p. 35.

9. <u>New Africa</u>, No. 137 (January, 1979), p. 14.

10. For a detailed report, see <u>The Weekly Review</u> (January 26, 1979), pp. 11-15; see also, <u>To the Point</u>, Vol. IIX, No. 5 (February 2, 1979), p. 36.

11. <u>To the Point</u>, Vol. VII, No. 45 (November 10, 1978), p. 51; <u>New Africa</u>, No. 142 (June, 1979), p. 48; <u>Washington</u>

<u>Post</u>, January 16, 1979, p. A14.

12. <u>New York Times</u>, November 1, 1978, p. 64; <u>To the Point</u>, Vol. VII, No. 45 (November 10, 1978), p. 51.

13. <u>New York Times</u>, November 2, 1978, p. 2.

14. <u>Ibid</u>, November 3, 1978, p. 16.

15. As one commentary noted, Nyerere "particularly resent-[ed] the fact that the white regimes of southern Africa were using Amin as an example of the failure of black African leadership." See "The Talk of the Town," <u>The New Yorker</u> (April 30, 1979), p. 31.

16. See the cogent analysis by John Darnton in <u>The New York Times</u>, March 12, 1979, p. 3.

17. See Sanford J. Ungar, "Tanzania Goes to War," <u>The New Republic</u>, Vol. CXXC, No. 10 (March 10, 1979), p. 17.

18. <u>Ibid</u>., p. 16; <u>New York Times</u>, November 6, 1978, p. 50.

19. <u>New York Times</u>, November 5, 1978, p. 5; <u>Africa</u>, Vol. IIX, No. 5 (February 2, 1979), p. 36.

20. <u>New York Times</u>, November 7, 1978, p. 5.

21. <u>To the Point</u>, Vol. VII, No. 51 (December 22, 1978), p. 33.

22. See David B. Ottaway, "Tanzanian Action to Unseat Amin Sets African Precedent," <u>Washington Post</u>, March 31, 1979, p. A22.

23. <u>New York Times</u>, November 9, 1978, p. 11.

24. <u>Ibid</u>., November 16, 1978, p. 6.

25. <u>Ibid</u>., November 28, 1978, p. 2.

26. Data in this section drawn from <u>The Military Balance</u>, <u>1978-1979</u> (London: The International Institute for Strategic Studies, 1978), p. 50; <u>New Africa</u>, No. 142

(June, 1979), pp. 48-49.

27. New York Times, March 25, 1979, Sec. IV, p. 3.

28. See The Weekly Review (March 9, 1979), p. 5.

29. See New Africa, No. 137 (January, 1979), p. 12.

30. Quoted in African Affairs, No. 92 (April, 1979), p. 37.

31. On rebel operations, see Financial Times (London), February 28, 1979 and February 6, 1979; Egyptian Gazette, February 15, 1979; Daily News (Tanzania), February 28, Gemini News Service Limited, February 27, 1979.

32. See The Standard (Kenya), March 2, 1979; Guardian (London), March 20, 1979; Economist, March 24, 1979.

33. See reports in Guardian, April 4, 1979; Daily Nation (Nairobi), April 9, 1979.

34. Gemini News Service, February 27, 1979.

35. See Daily News, January 12 and 19, 1979.

36. Ibid.

37. To further throttle Amin, the Tanzanians urged Kenya to close her border with Uganda. Nairobi's reply was that as a signatory to the Convention of Landlocked Countries, she had no right to deny Uganda essential military or economic supplies. As our concluding section will point out, there was more to this denial than strict adherence to international law. See in this regard The Standard, April 2, 1979; Guardian, April 2, 1979; New York Times, November 8, 1978, p. A7.

38. See The Weekly Review (March 9, 1979), pp. 6-7; New York Times, April 8, 1979, Sec. IV, p. 2. See also African Research Bulletin (February 1-28, 1979), p. 5154.

39. See Daily News, March 28, 1979. As The Weekly Review reports it, the Ugandan exiles assembled in Moshi firmly opposed Obote to head the organization; and the Tan-

zanians who up to then had firmly backed the former president, abided by their wishes. The Weekly Review (April 6, 1979), p. 6.

40. New York Times, April 11, 1979, p. 5.

41. Cited originally in Frederick L. Schuman, International Politics, 5th ed. (New York: McGraw-Hill, 1953), p. 261. Immediate source, Kenneth N. Waltz, Man the State and War (New York: Columbia University Press, 1959), pp. 187-88.

42. The Christian Science Monitor, July 17, 1979, p. 9.

43. Ibid.; The Warterly Economic Review of Tanzania, Mozambique, Annual Supplement, 1979, p. 12.

44. Ungar, "Tanzania Goes to War," p. 17.

45. Nye, Pan-Africanism and East African Integration, p. 250.

CHAPTER IX

Conclusion

Richard Fredland

To borrow from our colleagues in medicine, this volume has been essentially a post-mortem--both in time and intent. Several papers in this volume originated as components of a professional meeting panel, as mentioned in Chapter I, examining the demise of the EAC in 1977. And it was the demise which stimulated the preparation of this volume. Had the patient continued to survive, albeit in poor health, this probably would not have materialized. Consequently, there appears to be a logical dual purpose in a summary for the collection. First, I shall synthesize the collected diagnoses which have been offered regarding the collapse of the Community, and then I shall offer a sparser collection of lessons which we may have learned from the experience. Perhaps the wisest approach is that of Hazlewood who concludes with a long and penetrating list of questions--rather than answers--suggested by the present situation.

There is a strong temptation to compare the Community with the single extant institution which displays most persuasively the ostensible objectives integration is intended to achieve: The European Community. But as is detailed in virtually every comparative mention of international integration efforts, the differences between the two are far greater than the similarities. To look for lessons from East Africa by examining the successes of Europe would serve little useful purpose and would likely result in distorting whatever understanding this volume has succeeded in imparting. That temptation, then shall be resisted.

The problems confronted by the Community can be seen in several aspects. First, there were those institutional realities inherited from the British colonial system. There were political difficulties which arose during the life of the community, both because of internal decisions as to development objectives and the implications thereof, as well as responses to external events. There were externally-induced problems. And finally there were economic and financial problems. As should be now be clear, not only are these problems not discrete and available to be lifted up for specific scrutiny, but also, there is not complete agreement among the authors in this volume about which factors did indeed eventuate in the collapse of the Community nor about the relative importance of individual factors. In synthesizing those factors which have appeared in the several analytical

chapters preceding, I have attempted to deal with them objectively, having already had an opportunity to express my
views in one of the chapters. Here follows, then, an evaluation of factors which caused, or contributed to the demise
of, the East African Community. Their explication has taken
place in one or more of the preceding chapters.

The category of institutional weaknesses probably encom-
passes as many perceived faults as any other single grouping.
Every author identified problems in this category, and the
listing crosses all the other types of categorization which
is possible. The simple fact that there had been three pre-
existing polities, though under British pressure to consolidate, defines a large area of problems. The concentration
of economic as well as other types of activity in Kenya during the British period put the other two partners at a permanent disadvantage. And even with the conscious dispersal
of some of the services and corporate headquarters, the aura
of a dominant Kenya prevailed.

The Treaty was, necessarily, timid in what it proposed,
being a voluntary exercise opposed to the British compulsion
to integrate. Because three sovereign political entities
were agreeing to tie their futures to one another, there was
political reticence. Consequently, the objectives of the
Community were not clearly set out. This was tied to the
eventual unwillingness of the members to participate in joint
fiscal or industrial planning. With the decision-making retained by the three Presidents, the bureaucracy, which had
begun typically on a wave of enthusiasm, was circumscribed.
As hostilities emerged among the Authority, solutions faded
and problems ascended.

The assumed commitment on the part of some was not
shared by others. Especially as perceptions regarding relative benefits changed was there increased resistence to--or
divergence from--common policies.

Particularly was this apparent in viewing development
experiences in the three members. Kenya began in first place
and proceeded to consolidate that position through superior
levels of foreign investment, exploitation of her central
location, positive external reinforcement of her capitalist
system, and reinforcement from these advantages in the forms

of tourism and international respectability.

Integration theory is generally firm on the matter of popular perception of benefits: If the citizens of participating member states do not <u>perceive</u> benefits from their participation--it is virtually unquestioned that costs will be quite visible--it is unlikely that participation can be contained. Ravenhill especially emphasizes this. Certainly this is true in a participatory political system or in a situation, perhaps such as Kenya, in which the potential for political instability lies relatively close to the surface. So, as costs continued, generally in the form of constraints on unilateral decision-making, and benefits appeared to be less and less clearcut, the political desirability to withdraw grew. This reached irresistable proportions with the absolute collapse of the Ugandan economy under Amin, Kenya's increasing fear of aggression to her North, and Tanzania's dual problems of a lagging development program and enticements to the South.

Institutionally, the Community was hampered by the inherent problems of dispersed agencies, a poor decision-making mechanism, and a lack of coordinated planning. All of these were, in a way, secondary problems which stemmed from even more basic factors.

Political problems, while not distinct from others, can be mentioned as another category. The hostility between Presidents Nyerere and Amin prevented the convening of the Authority, though it is argued that had the requisite "political will" existed problems could have been dealt with by consensus achieved at a lower bureaucratic level. The ideological disparity between especially Kenya and Tanzania exacerbated relations which might have otherwise been smoothed over. But in applying their differing perspectives to common Community activities, little common ground for cooperation resulted. Similarly, the need to flex political muscles necessitated, ipso facto, separate paths. The cumulative effect of the build-up of problems made attempts at solution-- much less the solution itself--increasingly difficult till finally the weight of that burden overwhelmed the political ability of the system to survive.

Particularly Uganda and Tanzania experienced internal

problems, essentially economic, but which were translated into political expression within the Community. The failure of President Nyerere's Ujamaa program resulted in the need for political diversions. The collapse of the Uganda infrastructure under Amin led to a variety of political responses both within and without that beleaguered country. The ultimate vulnerability of Uganda was demonstrated in the 1978-79 war with Tanzania discussed by Gregorian.

Particular economic and financial problems plagued the Community. The transfer tax which was intended to offset the development imbalance between Kenya and the other two partners--as was discriminatory treatment against Kenya by the Development Bank--failed to achieve its objective. Undoubtedly one of the underlying economic problems, both theoretically as well as historically, was the limited benefits a common market can bring to developing countries which, necessarily, do not have complementary economies. The potential from trade among the members was easily offset by the established trading patterns with and technological needs from industrialized states. Coupling this with, for example, Tanzania's dependence upon capital or credit transfers (as Africa's number one aid recipient) before trade transpired, it is apparent that an East African common trading area has limited potential at best. As the community operated, Kenya's persistent balance of payments surplus within the Community became increasingly unacceptable. With the complete absence of coordinated industrial planning, the effects of whatever benefits there might have been were not spread among the members, despite the customs union.

Other economic concerns included the persistent national balance of payment disequilibria Tanzania and Uganda experienced outside the Community as well as with Kenya. Further, the fear of a socialist regime in Uganda was a factor in Kenyan-Ugandan relations both during the Obote regime as well as at the time of Amin's demise.

The unequal distribution of benefits among the Community members is essentially an economic concern, but it deserves special mention. While cognizance has been taken in the establishment of the Community (e.g., the transfer tax) as well as in the operation of the East African Development Bank of the unequal development levels among the three participants, the outcome of Community operation bore out unfavorable results nonetheless. For example, there was distinctly uneven foreign investment which favored Kenya. These as well as other developments not surprisingly resulted in changing perceptions of the benefits being generated by the Community--which quickly was translated into a kind of political anemia regarding the Community. The ultimate example of unequal distribution of benefits came with Kenya's profiteering from Uganda's collapsed and isolated economy during the last years of the Community through the period of the Tanzanian-Ugandan war.

Finally, there were external problems--again, not totally divorced from the preceding. As Amin became increasingly dependent upon external support, particularly from Libya, his flexibility regarding the Community shrank, a factor which mattered less and less as Uganda's economy decayed to the point of being inconsequential in the Community. In the final stages of this collapse extralegal relations with Kenya outweighed recognized economic intercourse.

Similarly, during the last years of the Community, Tanzania was distracted from the Community. From 1965, with Rhodesia's Unilateral Declaration of Independence, Mozambique's revolution, and other related developments in Southern Africa, President Nyerere played a leadership role at the international level in seeking an African solution to problems which portended significant great power interest. This undoubtedly affected President Nyerere's perception of how to apportion his energies--the positive movement to the South apparently triumped. Simultaneously, Tanzania was the beneficiary of Chinese interest through the construction of the Tazara Railway which, in linking Tanzania and Zambia, further eroded her commitment to the Community.

As Tanzania was seen, especially by the United States, as being increasingly seduced into the Eastern camp, and with Soviet maneuvering in the Persian Gulf and Horn areas, the United States was increasingly interested in maintaining a strong relationship with Kenya. As both the Horn and southern Africa destabilized in the mid- and late 1970's external pressures further increased preventing the coincidence of foreign policies of Community members. And while Uganda benefited, if in a perverse way, from Libyan oil wealth, the increase in oil prices in the 1970's imposed financial strains upon the Community for which it had no means of compensating.

Assertions, as pointed out by Potholm, that there were, in effect, neo-colonial machinations to support external interests which were not concerned with the success of the Community cannot be overlooked. Geopolitical and economic interests of the superpowers and former colonial metropoles unquestionably affected the international climate in which the three Community members operated. The net effect of those international relations could have been more or less supportive of the Community. And, deductively at least one must conclude that disintegrative forces were increasing.

Having examined the myriad problems which beset the Community throughout its decade of operation, one is obliged to make something of the shambles that remains. Both in the interest of rising above sterile scholarship irrelevant to providing guidance to those who might formulate policy for future integration attempts as well as for those who want to better predict the potential of other integration attempts, a survey of the consequences of the Community is desirable.

The implications of the collapse of the Community were less significant than they might have been had the institutions been stronger and the member states more dependent upon them for the services and policy they were originally intended to provide. However, as the Community shriveled the dependence of the member states upon Community services and infrastructure declined virtually to the vanishing point so that the transfer of functions from the Community to at least Kenya and Tanzania occurred with virtually no disruption. The majority of the burden of transition was borne by those Community bureaucrats who were at the Headquarters in Arusha, Tanzania, and had difficulty in obtaining their pay and accomplishing repatriation, especially to a barbarous and convulsive Uganda.

Economically, there was the immediate effect--which from another time and perspective could be seen as a cause--of a stagnation in tourism. The Tanzanian parks were closed, but the Nairobi hotels were open--leading the Kenyans, of course, to redirect their clients to the somewhat less spectacular

Kenyan game parks, apparently with some success. With the closure of borders, whatever economies of scale achieved through the Community were lost, and particularly did Kenyan manufacturers and distributors experience a shrinkage of markets, though expansion beyond former Community borders should more than offset that.

The need for regional industrial planning was again clearly demonstrated as perhaps the most significant policy area as each country embarked on individual development programs leading, undoubtedly, to redundant development if not controlled by some level of agreement. This, absent the buffering of the Community, would render these industries more vulnerable to international competition.

Politically, there is always the potential benefit within any state of proclaiming an external threat followed by the need to consolidate the home forces. If threat is permitted to escalate, there is the potential for an East African arms race, especially so long as Kenya perceives territorial ambitions on the part of her northern neighbors. Disillusionment with hopes gone awry may increase the political cost for any subsequent venture.

Within the several partner states, the direction of political will becomes a question. After a decade of drumming up support for the Community, where can this body of allegiance be directed? And once it is spent on national or subnational goals, at what price can it be re-established if and when a new supranational effort arises? At a less significant level it can be expected that a certain measure of erosion can be experienced as the citizens of the states first are directed toward the virtues of the Community and then rather abruptly redirected against former allies. In circumstances which are already uncertain, this added uncertainty can produce unfortunate political ennui.

Finally, not that any prescient observer of the international scene needs the reminder, the lesson can be readily learned that there is a price to be paid for disorder--particuarly the dissolution of political order in Uganda in this case. As has been observed earlier, it is difficult to ascribe the failure of the Community to any single factor, but rather to a combination of several negatives. For every

200

fault, had there been a solution, the incremental negativism described by one author, might have been incremental integration and the Community might have survived. The European Community has thur far found that it can indeed weather substantial storms because the integrative commitment exceeds the disintegrative propensities. On the other hand, the United States in its founding years found the opposite--that a complete halt and beginning again was the desirable response to centrifugal-centripetal disorder in its political community.

With regard to lessons which might productively be drawn for similar behaviors in other developing areas, the evidence is inconclusive. As with the enumeration of questions by Hazlewood, there are more unknowns than knowns. It is not clear that East Africa's developing economic circumstances per se contributed inordinately to the demise of the Community. Certainly, in the case of many factors, their impact was exacerbated because of the level of development. But it would be an overstatement to identify "underdevelopedness" as the key.

The most important single consideration in this vein was the absence of complementarity of economic systems. The absence of political will which would have presumably led to coordinated industrial development was exacerbated by many similar aspects of the three economies. This is especially vivified when the East African Community is compared to the relatively robust European Community. when viewed from the national perspective--which the Community, not surprisingly, did not rise above--economic activity was seen as primarily competitive, not cooperative. Only through the effective surrender of economic, and effectively political, decision-making can a common market cum integrative institution move beyond the talking stage to effective action. The Community never reached that level.

The vulnerability of developing states to external forces puts them in a category apart from more established economies and polities in terms of decision-making across a wide spectrum of issues. The neo-colonialist involvements of several states in East Africa constrained the development potential, especially in the industrial area, which is where the most immediate potential for visible benefit rested. And without that popular support potential, the necessary political will could not be cultivated to bear the implicit costs of any such effort. Perhaps here is one of the clearest lessons for developing area integration efforts: Build into the projected institution some readily apparent benefits which will presumably lead to popular support for the further development of the infrastructure and the bearing of the political costs which are inevitable in any such venture. This is no less important in mature economic systems, but the fragility of economic life in developing areas requires, for even routine political support, substantial positive political feedback to retain adequate allegiance.

Obiously the lesson of problems stemming from the number of parties involved is simple to correct. United Nations-instigated discussions about a new and larger East African integration effort positively address this problem. At the same time, of course, the disintegrative potential of attempting to align a large number of disparate polities presents another hazard. the simple conclusion is that this possible "wave of the future" can be led in only with great difficulty.

Whatever has happened, there is certainly enough that has been learned about the East African Community that it would be able to begin again in whatever manifestation free of many of the political and economic albatrosses which were integral to its demise. Certainly, it has not disproved the validity of integration efforts in developing areas.

BIBLIOGRAPHY

Africa Confidential. "East African Community: What is Left?"
  Africa Confidential 18(7) April, 1977, pp. 4-5.
Alker, Hayward R. Jr. "Integration Logics: A Review,
  Extension and Critique," in Lindberg and Scheingold (eds.)
  Regional Integration, pp. 265-310.
Amin, N. M. "Enlargement of the East African Community
  Particularly with Respect to Zambian Application,"
  Universities Social Science Council Conference, Makerere
  University, Kampala, 1971.
Axline, W. Andrew. "Underdevelopment, Dependence and Inte-
  gration: The Politics of Regionalism in the Third World,"
  International Organization 31(1) Winter, 1977, pp. 83-105.
Ballance, Frank C. Zambia and the East African Community.
  Syracuse: Syracuse University Program of East African
  Studies, 1971.
Balassa, Bela and Ardy Stoutjesdik. "Economic Integration
  Among Developing Countries," Journal of Common Market
  Studies XIV(1) September, 1975, pp. 37-55.
Banfield, Jane. "The Structure and Administration of the
  East African Common Services Organization," in Leys and
  Robson (eds.) Federation in East Africa, pp. 30-40.
Beck, Ann. "The East African Community and Regional Research
  in Science and Medicine," paper presented to the African
  Studies Association, Philadelphia, 1972.
Belshaw, D. G. R. "Agricultural Production and Trade in the
  East African Common Market," in Leys and Robson (eds.)
  Federation in East Africa, pp. 83-101.
Birch, A. H. "Opportunities and Problems of Federation,"
  in Leys and Robson (eds.) Federation in East Africa,
  pp. 6-29.
Boals, Kay. "The Concept 'Subordinate International System':
  A Critique," in Falk and Mendlovitz (eds.) Regional
  Politics and World Order, pp. 399-410.
Burke, F. G. "Unity and Diversity in East Africa--A
  Synthesisless Dialectic," paper presented at Duke
  University Commonwealth Studies Center, February, 1965.
Cantori, Louis J. and Steven L. Spiegel. "The International
  Relations of Regions," in Falk and Mendlovitz (eds.)
  Regional Politics and World Order, pp. 335-353.
Chidzero, B. T. G. "The Meaning of Economic Integration in
  Africa," East Africa Journal II(8) December, 1965, pp. 23-
  28.

Chime, Chimelu. Integration and Politics Among East African States; Limitations and Horizons of Mid-term Theorizing. Uppsala: The Scandinavian Institute of African Studies, 1977.

Cohen, John M. "Leadership Identity Problems and Regional Integration and Political Development," paper presented at Social Science Council Conference, Makerere University, Kampala, 1971.

Cox, Thomas S. "Development Assistance and Subregional Integration; Some Lessons from Donor Involvement with the East African Community," unpublished manuscript, February, 1979.

DeSmith, S. A. "Integration of Legal Systems," in Leys and Robson (eds.) Federation in East Africa, pp. 158-171.

Diamond, Peter A. "Effective Protection of the East African Transfer Taxes," East African Economics Review 4 (New Series) No. 2, December, 1968, pp. 37-48.

Doimi Di Delupis, Ingrid. The East African Community and Common Market. London: Longmans, 1970.

Dolan, Michael B. "Neofunctionalism: Problem Shift in a Theory of Regional Integration," papers of the Peace Science Society International, No. 25, 1975.

Dresang, Dennis L. and Ira Sharkansky. "Public Corporations in Single-Country and Regional Settings: Kenya and the East African Community," International Organization 27(3) Summer, 1973, pp. 303-328.

East African Common Services Organization, Report of the Africanisation Commission, n.p.:E.A.C.S.O., March, 1963.

_____. Treaty for East African Cooperation. Nairobi: Government Printer for E.A.C.S.O., 1967.

East African Community, Common Market and Economic Affairs Secretariat. Review of Economic Integration within the East African Community 1973-74. Arusha: East African Community, May, 1974.

_____. East African Court of Appeal, Annual Report to 1975.

_____. East African Customs and Excise Department. Annual Trade Reports. Yearly to 1974.

_____. East African Statistical Department, Economic and Statistical Review. Quarterly to November 1975.

_____. East African Statistical Department, Statistical Survey of the East African Community Institutions. Yearly to 1974.

El-Ayouty, Yassin and Hugh Brooks (eds.). Africa and International Organization. The Hague: Martinus Nijhoff, 1974.

Elkan, Peter G. "Measuring the Impact of Economic Integration Among Developing Countries," Journal of Common Market Studies XIV(1) September, 1975, pp. 55-68.

Eze, Osita C. The Legal Status of Foreign Investments in the East African Common Market. Leiden: A.W. Sijthoff, 1975.

Falk, Richard A. and Saul H. Mendlovitz (eds.) Regional Politics and World Order. San Francisco: W. H. Freeman, 1973.

Franck, Thomas M. East African Unity Through Law. New Haven: Yale University Press, 1964.

Gappert, Gary. "Regional Planning in East Africa," East Africa Journal V(6) June, 1968, pp. 30-34.

Ghai, Dharam P. "State Trading and Regional Economic Integration: The East African Experience," Journal of Common Market Studies XII(3) 1974, pp. 296-318.

_____. "Territorial Distribution of the Benefits and Costs of the East African Common Market," in Leys and Robson (eds.) Federation in East Africa, pp. 72-82.

Ghai, Yash P. "East African Industrial Licensing System: A Device for the Regional Allocation of Industry," Journal of Common Market Studies XII(3) 1974, pp. 265-295.

_____. "Legal Aspects of the Treaty for East African Co-operation," East African Economic Review 3 (New Series) No. 2, December, 1967, pp. 27-38.

_____. "Some Legal Aspects of an East African Federation," in Leys and Robson (eds.) Federation in East Africa, pp. 172-182.

Gitelson, Susan Aurelia. "Can the U.N. be an Effective Catalyst for Regional Integration? The Case of the East African Community," Journal of Developing Areas 8(1) October, 1973, pp. 65-82.

Green, Reginald H. "Economic Union in East Africa: Principles, Prices, and Proceeds," paper presented at East African Institute of Social Research Conference, Makerere University College, Kampala, January, 1966.

Green, Reginald H. and Ann Seidman. Unity or Poverty? The Economics of Pan-Africanism. Harmondsworth: Penguin, 1968.

Gregg, Robert W. "The U.N. Regional Economic Commissions and Integration in the Underdeveloped Regions," International Organization XX(2) Spring, 1966, reprinted in Nye (ed.) International Regionalism, pp. 304-332.

Gruhn, Isebill V. Functionalism in Africa: Scientific and Technical Integration, unpublished Ph.D. dissertation, U.C. Berkeley, 1967.

Gruhn, Isebill V. "The Lome Convention: Inching Towards Interdependence," _International Organization_ 30(2) Spring, 1976, pp. 241-262.

Grundemann, H. E. "Industrial Development in East Africa; An Appraisal Including Possibilities for Future Acceleration," paper presented at Universities Social Science Conference, Makerere University, Kampala, 1971.

Guruli, Kassim. "Towards an Independent and Equal East African Common Market," _East Africa Journal_ 8(9) September, 1971, pp. 25-32.

Haas, Ernst B. "Is There a Hole in the Whole? Knowledge, Technology, Interdependence and the Construction of International Regimes," _International Organization_ 29(3) Summer, 1975, pp. 827-876.

_____. _The Obsolescence of Regional Integration Theory._ Berkeley: Institute of International Studies, University of California, Berkeley, Research Series No. 25, 1975.

_____. "The Study of Regional Integration: Reflections on the Joy and Anguish of Pre-Theorizing," in Lindberg and Scheingold (eds.) _Regional Integration: Theory and Research_, pp. 3-42.

_____. "Turbulent Fields and the Theory of Regional Integration," _International Organization_ 30(2) Spring, 1976, pp. 173-212.

_____. "The Uniting of Europe and the Uniting of Latin America," _Journal of Common Market Studies_ V(4) June, 1967, pp. 315-343.

Haas, Ernst B. and Philippe C. Schmitter. "Economics and Differential Patterns of Political Integration: Projections About Unity in Latin America," _International Organization_ 18(4) Autumn, 1964, pp. 705-737.

Hall, Marshall and Dhiru Tanna. "Comments on Exchange Rate Unification," paper presented at Universities Social Science Conference, Makerere University, Kampala, 1971.

_____. "Equality in the East African Common Market: A Reply," _East Africa Journal_ IX(2) February, 1972, pp. 35-39.

Hammond, Robert C. _Fiscal Harmonization in the East African Community._ Amsterdam: International Bureau of Fiscal Documentation, 1975.

Hansen, Roger D. "Regional Integration: Reflections on a Decade of Theoretical Efforts," _World Politics_ XXI(2) January, 1969, pp. 242-271.

Hazlewood, Arthur (ed.) _African Integration and Disintegration._ London: Oxford University Press, 1967.

Hazlewood, Arthur. "An Approach to the Analysis of the Spatial Distribution of the Market in East Africa," Bulletin of the Oxford University Institute of Economics and Statistics 31(4) November, 1969, pp. 243-261.

_____. "The Coordination of Transport Policy," in Leys and Robson (eds.) Federation in East Africa, pp. 111-123.

_____. "The East African Common Market: Importance and Effects," Bulletin of the Oxford University Institute of Economics and Statistics 28(1) February, 1966, pp. 1-18.

_____. Economic Integration: The East African Experience. London: Heinemann, 1975.

_____. "The Kampala Treaty and the Accession of New Members to the East African Community," East African Economic Review 4(2) December, 1968, pp. 49-63.

_____. "Notes on the Treaty for East African Cooperation," East African Economic Review 3 (New Series) No. 2, December, 1967, pp. 63-80.

_____. "The 'Shiftability' of Industry and the Measurement of Gains and Losses in the East African Common Market," Bulletin of the Oxford University Institute of Economics and Statistics 28(2) May, 1966, pp. 63-72.

Helleiner, G. K. "Transfer Taxes, Tariffs and the East African Common Market," East African Economic Review 3 (New Series), No. 2, December, 1967, pp. 53-61.

Hoffman, Stanley. "Obstinate or Obsolete? The Fate of the Nation State and the Case of Western Europe," Daedalus 95(3) Summer, 1966, reprinted in Nye (ed.) International Regionalism, pp. 177-230.

Hughes, A. J. East Africa: The Search for Unity. Revised Edition. Harmondsworth: Penguin, 1969.

Inkeles, Alex. "The Emerging Social Structure of the World," World Politics XXVII(4) July, 1975, pp. 467-495.

Jacob, Philip E. and James V. Toscano (eds.) The Integration of Political Communities. Philadelphia: J.B. Lippincott, 1964.

Jalloh, Abdul A. Political Integration in French-Speaking Africa. Berkeley: Institute of International Studies, University of California, Research Series #20, 1973.

Kato, L. L. "East African Associates and the European Economic Community," East Africa Journal 8(6) June, 1971, pp. 7-13.

Keen, B. A. "The East African Agricultural and Forestry Research Organization; Its Origins and Objectives," Nairobi: East African Standard, Ltd., n.d.

Keohane, Robert O. and Joseph S. Nye. "International Interdependence and Integration," in Fred I. Greenstein and Nelson W. Polsby (eds.) Handbook of Political Science Vol. 8 International Politics. Reading, Mass.: Addison-Wesley Pub. Co., 1975, pp. 363-414.

Keohane, Robert O. and Joseph S. Nye. Power and Inter-
    dependence: World Politics in Transition. Boston: Little
    Brown, 1977.
_____. "Transgovernmental Relations and International
    Organizations," World Politics XXVII(9) October, 1974,
    pp. 39-62.
Kurtz, Donn M. "Political Integration in Africa: The Mali
    Federation," Journal of Modern African Studies 8(3)
    October, 1970, pp. 405-424.
Leys, Colin and Peter Robson (eds.). Federation in East
    Africa: Opportunities and Problems. Nairobi: Oxford
    University Press, 1965.
Lindberg, Leon N. "Political Integration as a Multidimensional
    Phenomenon Requiring Multivariate Measurement," in Lindberg
    and Scheingold (eds.) Regional Integration, pp. 45-127.
Lindberg, Leon N. and Stuart A. Scheingold (eds.) Regional
    Integration: Theory and Research. Cambridge: Harvard
    University Press, 1971.
Low, D. A. and Alison Smith (eds.). History of East Africa.
    Oxford: Clarendon Press, 1976.
Low, D. and J. M. Lonsdale. "Introduction: Towards the New
    Order 1945-63," in Low and Smith (eds.) History of East
    Africa Volume III, pp. 1-63.
Malecela, John S. "What Next for the East African Community:
    The Case for Integration," The African Review 2(1) June,
    1972, pp. 211-217.
Massell, Benton F. East African Economic Union: An Evaluation
    and Some Implications for Policy. Santa Monica: Rand
    Corporation Memorandum RM-3880-RC, December, 1963.
Mazrui, Ali A. "Tanzaphilia," Transition, 31, 1967.
Mazzeo, Domenico. Foreign Assistance and the East African
    Common Services 1960-1970 with Special Reference to Multi-
    lateral Contributions. Munich: Weltforum Verlag, 1975.
Mboya, T. J. "East African Labour Policy and Federation," in
    Leys and Robson (eds.) Federation in East Africa, pp. 102-110
Mead, Donald C. "Economic Cooperation in East Africa," paper
    presented at African Studies Association, Los Angeles, 1968.
Miller, Lynn H. "The Prospects for Order Through Regional
    Security," in Falk and Mendlovitz (eds.) Regional Politics
    and World Order, pp. 50-74.
Morse, Edward L. "The Politics of Interdependence," Inter-
    national Organization 23(2) Spring, 1969, pp. 311-326.
Mytelka, Lynn K. "The Salience of Gains in Third World
    Intergrative Systems," World Politics XXV(2) January, 1973,
    pp. 236-250.

Nabudere, D. Wadada. "The Transport System in East Africa," paper presented at Universities Social Science Council Conference, Makerere University, Kampala, 1971.

Nazareth, J. M. "Proposed Association of East African Federalists," paper presented at Universities Social Science Council Conference, Makerere University, Kampala, 1971.

Nedgwa, Philip. The Common Market and Development in East Africa, 2nd Edition. Nairobi: East African Publishing House, 1968.

_____. "Development Effects of the East African Common Market," paper presented at East Africa Institute of Social Research, Makerere University, Kampala, January, 1975.

Newlyn, W. T. "Gains and Losses in the East African Common Market," Yorkshire Bulletin of Economic and Social Research 17(2) November, 1965, pp. 130-138.

_____. "The Significance of Separate Monetary Systems in East Africa," paper presented at East Africa Institute of Social Research, Makerere University, Kampala, 1966.

Newman, Peter. "The Economics of Integration in East Africa," in Leys and Robson (eds.) Federation in East Africa. Nairobi: Oxford University Press, 1965, pp. 56-71.

Nixson, F. I. "The East African Common Market: Historical Development and Current Problems," paper presented at East Africa Institute of Social Research, Makerere University, Kampala, 1971.

Nsibambi, Apolo Robin. "Political Commitment and Economic Integration: East Africa's Experience," The African Review 2(1) June, 1972, pp. 189-210.

Nye, Joseph S., Jr. "Attitudes of Makerere Students Toward the East African Federation," paper presented at East African Institute of Social Research, Kivokoni College, Dar Es Salaam, January, 1963.

_____. "Central American Regional Integration," in Nye (ed.) International Regionalism, pp. 377-429.

_____. "Comparing Common Markets: A Revised Neo-Functionalist Model," in Lindberg and Scheingold (eds.) Regional Integration, pp. 192-231.

_____. "The Extent and Viability of East African Cooperation," in Leys and Robson (eds.) Federation in East Africa, pp. 40-55.

_____. International Regionalism: Readings. Boston: Little Brown, 1968.

_____. Pan-Africanism and East African Integration. Cambridge, Mass.: Harvard University Press, 1965.

_____. "Patterns and Catalysts in Regional Integration," International Organization XIX(4) August, 1965, reprinted in Nye (ed.) International Regionalism, pp. 333-349.

Nye, Joseph S., Jr. Peace in Parts: Integration and Conflict in Regional Organization. Boston: Little Brown, 1971.

Obol-Ochola, James Y. "The Executives of the EAC, EEC, and LAFTA: A Comparative Institutional Study of the Dichotomy of National Leadership and Regional Economic Dependence," paper presented at Social Science Council Conference, Makerere University, 1971.

Odhiambo, T. R. "The Crisis of Science in East Africa," East Africa Journal II(11) April, 1966, pp. 3-29.

Ojow, Francis. "EADB and the Industrial Development of EA," 1971 Universities Social Science Council Conference, Makerere University, Kampala.

Pentland, Charles. International Theory and European Integration. New York: Free Press, 1973.

Rake, Allan. "Can East Africa Take the Strain," African Development 8(10) October, 1974, pp. 15-18.

Reinton, Per Olav. "International Structure and International Integration: The Case of Latin America," Journal of Peace Research 4, 1967, pp. 334-365.

Richards, C. G. "The EA Literature Bureau," in UNESCO Bulletin for Libraries, XV(5) September/October, 1961.

Robson, Peter. Economic Integration in Africa. London: George Allen and Unwin, 1968.

_____. "Federal Finance," in Leys and Robson (eds.) Federation in East Africa, pp. 124-144.

_____. "The Re-Shaping of East African Cooperation," East African Economic Review 3 (New Series), No. 2, December, 1967, pp. 1-11.

Robson, Peter and D. A. Lury. The Economics of Africa. Evanston, Illinois: Northwestern University Press, 1969.

Roe, Allan R. "The Impact of the East African Treaty on the Distribution of E.A.C.S.O. Benefits," East African Economic Review 3 (New Series) No. 2, December, 1967, pp. 39-52.

_____. "The Re-Shaping of East African Economic Cooperation," East Africa Journal 4(5) August, 1967, pp. 11-16.

_____. "Terms of Trade and Transfer Effects in the East African Common Market: An Empirical Study," Bulletin of the Oxford University Institute of Economics and Statistics 31(3) August, 1969, pp. 153-167.

Rosberg, Carl G. with Aaron Segal. "An East African Federation," International Conciliation #545, May, 1963.

Rosecrance, Richard and Arthur Stein. "Interdependence: Myth or Reality," World Politics 26(1) October, 1973, pp. 1-27.

Rothchild, Donald. The EAC. An expanded and updated version of a paper published in the EA Economic Review, Vol. III, No. 2, December, 1967.

Rothchild, Donald. "From Hegemony to Bargaining in East African Relations," Journal of African Studies 1(4) Winter, 1974, pp. 390-416.

_____. Politics of Integration: An East African Documentary. Nairobi: East African Publishing House, 1968.

_____. "The Political Implications of the Treaty," East African Economic Review 3 (New Series), No. 2, December, 1967, pp. 13-26.

_____. Toward Unity in Africa. Washington: Public Affairs Press, 1960.

Russett, Bruce M. "International Regions and the International System," in Falk and Mendlovitz (eds.) Regional Politics and World Order, pp. 182-202.

Saith, S. A. "The EA School of Librarianship," article in Encyclopaedia of Library and Information Science, Vol. 7 New York: Dekker, 1972 (Allen Kent and Harold Lancour, eds.).

Scheingold, Stuart A. "Domestic and International Consequences of Regional Integration," in Lindberg and Scheingold (eds.) Regional Integration: Theory and Research, pp. 372-398.

Schmitter, Philippe C. "Central American Integration: Spill-Over, Spill-Around or Encapsulation?" Journal of Common Market Studies IX(1) September, 1970, pp. 1-48.

_____. "A Revised Theory of Regional Integration," in Lindberg and Scheingold (eds.) Regional Integration: Theory and Research, pp. 232-264.

Segal, Aaron. East Africa: Strategy for Economic Cooperation. Nairobi: East African Institute of Social and Cultural Affairs, African Contemporary Monographs #1, 1965.

_____. "The Integration of Developing Countries: Some Thoughts on East Africa and Central America," Journal of Common Market Studies 5(3) March, 1967, pp. 252-282.

Seidman, Ann. Comparative Development Strategies in East Africa. Nairobi: East African Publishing House, 1972.

Shaw, Timothy M. "Regional Cooperation and Conflict in Africa," International Journal 30(4) Autumn, 1975, pp. 671-688.

Syracuse University. "Papers on the East African Community," Syracuse University: Maxwell Graduate School of Citizenship and Public Affairs, Program of East African Studies, Occasional Paper #47, 1968.

Tandon, Yashpal. "The EACM: A Perspective from 1971," 1971 East African University Social Science Conference, Kampala, paper #22.

Tandon, Yash and Ali A. Mazrui. "The East African Community as a Sub-Regional Grouping," in El-Ayouty and Brooks (eds.) Africa and International Organization, pp. 182-205.

Tanzania, Government of. _Economic Survey_. Annually until
    1975.
Tanzania, Ministry of Information and Tourism. _Meetings and_
    Discussions on the Proposed East African Federation. Dar
    Es Salaam: Government Printer, September, 1964.
Tharp, Paul A. Jr. (ed.) _Regional International Organizations_:
    Structures and Functions. New York: St. Martins Press, 1971
Van Arkadie, B. "Central Banking in an East African Federation
    in Leys and Robson (eds.) _Federation in East Africa_, pp. 14
    157.
Viner, Jacob. _The Customs Union Issue_. London: Stevens and
    Sons, Ltd., 1950.
Waltz, Kenneth N. "The Myth of National Interdependence," in
    Charles Kindleberger (ed.) _The International Corporation_:
    A Symposium. Cambridge, Mass.: M.I.T. Press, 1970, pp.
    205-223.
Wionczek, M. S. "Economic Integration and Regional Distribution
    of Industrial Activities: A Comparative Study," _East African_
    Economic Review 2 (New Series) No. 1, June, 1966, pp. 55-68
    and Vol. 3 (New Series) No. 1, June, 1967, pp. 31-44.
————. "Requisites for Viable Economic Integration," in
    Nye (ed.) _International Regionalism_, pp. 287-303.
————. "The Rise and the Decline of Latin American Economic
    Integration," _Journal of Common Market Studies_ IX(1)
    September, 1970, pp. 49-66.
Wood, R. N. "The East African Common Market: A Reassessment,"
    Bulletin of the Oxford University Institute of Economics
    and Statistics 28(4) November, 1966, pp. 273-80.

Contributors

Richard Fredland is Chairman of the Political Science Department of Indiana University-Purdue University at Indianapolis where he has been on the faculty since 1970. He teaches in the area of international relations and is particularly interested in international organizations in Africa. In 1977 he was on sabbatical leave in Nairobi. He has recently completed a study of international relations in Africa published as <u>Africa Faces the World</u>. In 1973 an article on the Organization of African Unity appeared in <u>African Affairs</u>.

Hrach Gregorian, a doctoral candidate in the Politics Department, Brandeis University, is completing his Ph.D. thesis on congressional/executive relations and foreign policy making in the post-Vietnam period. He is the recipient of grants and fellowships from the Gulbenkian Foundation and the Gordon Foundation. He has taught at Boston College, Simmons college and the University of Massachusetts/Boston.

Arthur Hazlewood is currently Warden of Queen Elizabeth House, Oxford, and Director of the Oxford University Institute of Commonwealth Studies. He is also a Fellow of Pembroke College, Oxford, and has been its Vicegerent and Domestic Bursar. He was previously Senior Research Officer at the Oxford University Institute of Economics and Statistics. During the negotiation of the Treaty for East African Cooperation he was Director of the Common Market Secretariat in the President's Office in Kenya and subsequently he served as consultant to the East African Community, the East African Development Bank, and the Negotiating Team which dealt with applications from other countries to join the Community. His books on East African affairs include <u>Rail and Road in East Africa</u> (1964), <u>Economic Integration: The East African Experience</u> (1975), <u>Aid and Inequality in Kenya</u> (with G. Holtham, 1976), and <u>The Economy of Kenya: The Kenyatta Era</u> (1970).

Domenico Mazzeo is currently a lecturer on International Relations and International Organizations at the Department of Government and the Diplomacy Training Programme, University of Nairobi. His articles include "Les Nations Unies et la diplomatie de decolonisation" and "Foreign assistance and the East African Common Services". As part of a larger comparative study on intercountry cooperation in Africa and Latin America, he is currently carrying out research on "cooperation in science and technology in Africa".

Christian P. Potholm has traveled widely in Africa and written extensively about its politics. His books include, Four African Political Systems (1970), Swaziland: The Dynamics of Political Modernization (1972), Southern Africa in Perspective (1972), Liberation and Exploitation: The Struggle for Ethiopia (1976), and The Theory and Practice of African Politics (1978).

John Ravenhill, a doctoral candidate in the Department of Political Science, University of California, Berkeley, is affiliated with The Institute of International Studies. He previously taught at Makerere University, Uganda, and Indiana University. He has contributed articles and reviews to Africa Contemporary Record, Africa Studies Review, Canadian Journal of African Studies, International Journal, Journal of Commonwealth and Comparative Politics, and the Journal of Modern African Studies. Currently he is completing his doctoral dissertation, the subject of which is an evaluation of the Lome Convention.

Allen L. Springer is an instructor in the Department of Government and Legal Studies at Bowdoin College, Brunswick, Maine. A graduate of Amherst College and the Fletcher School of Law and Diplomacy, he specializes in international law and regional integration with an emphasis on environmental policy. He is the author of "Toward a Meaningful Concept of Pollution in International Law," which appeared in the International and Comparative Law Quarterly, and is presently at work on a study of the dispute between the United States and Canada over the proposed construction of major oil refinery at Eastport, Maine.